AF600642

THE CATHOLIC UNIVERSITY OF AMERICA
CANON LAW STUDIES
Number 61

CHURCH SUPPORT
IN THE
UNITED STATES

A DISSERTATION
Submitted to the Faculty of Canon Law of the Catholic University of America in Partial Fulfillment of the Requirements for the Degree of

DOCTOR OF CANON LAW

BY

MICHAEL N. KREMER, A.B., S.T.B., J.C.L.
Priest of the Diocese of St. Cloud

THE CATHOLIC UNIVERSITY OF AMERICA
WASHINGTON, D. C.
1930

Nihil Obstat

VALENTINUS SCHAAF, O.F.M., J.C.D.,
Censor Deputatus.
Washingtonii, D. C., die XXVII Maii, 1930.

Imprimatur

✠ JOSEPHUS FRANCISCUS BUSCH, D. D.,
Episcopus Sti. Clodoaldi.
Sti. Clodoaldi, die XXIX Maii, 1930.

COMPOSED BY
MONOTYPE COMPOSITION CO., INC.
BALTIMORE, MD.

TABLE OF CONTENTS

FOREWORD

The acquisition of sufficient material means for the effective prosecution of her work of salvation has always been an important and often perplexing problem for the Catholic Church in the United States. The reason for this is to be found in the novel conditions which the Church had to meet in this country. From a few scattered missions, without a single residential ordinary, which ministered to the spiritual needs of less than twenty thousand souls, she has, in less than a century and a half, developed into a magnificent army of twenty million Catholics under the spiritual jurisdiction of over a hundred archbishops and bishops.

The erection of the houses of worship, of the educational and charitable institutions of all kinds, to provide for the needs of this multitude, and the maintenance of the thousands of religious men and women who devoted themselves to a life of spiritual service, necessarily entailed the expenditure of huge sums of money. To obtain these means the Church in the United States has depended almost entirely upon the voluntary contributions of her children. In view of the fact that most of them have always belonged to the poorer members of society, their generous response to the Church's appeals is a glorious proof of the continued vitality of the Catholic Church in this country.

The methods by which these funds were raised are many and various. Remembering the desperate needs which had to be provided for, and the trying circumstances under which the clergy frequently labored, it is not surprising that dubious schemes were occasionally resorted to.

Although introduced with the best of intentions to provide for some pressing want, the nature of some of these methods and the dangers connected with them were such that the Church could not approve of their further employment.

The object of this brief study is to consider some of the problems connected with the support of religion in the light of the spirit and legislation of the Church. That it is not intended to be a complete and final exposition of the subject need not be mentioned. Discussion of Mass Stipends and Stole Fees, both of which are connected with the problem of Church support, has been entirely omitted, since both of these subjects have been ably treated in other works of this school. If this study but contributes its mite to the settlement of some problem, to the eradication of any possibly existing abuse or to the prevention of such in the future, the work will be amply repaid.

The writer takes this occasion to express his deep gratitude to his Right Reverend Bishop, Joseph F. Busch, D.D., for the opportunity of extended study and for his kindly interest and encouragement; to the Right Reverend Monsignor Thiebaut for many valuable suggestions and other kindnesses; to all the members of the Faculty of Canon Law at the Catholic University for their generous assistance and unfailing guidance; and to all who have in any way contributed to the production of this study.

CHAPTER ONE

Historical Conspectus of Church Support

1.—During the First Three Centuries

From the very beginning of her existence, the Church has relied upon the faithful to provide the temporal means which she has needed to carry on her work on earth. In doing this she has not introduced a new or unusual practice distinctive of the Christian religion. Ever since his creation, man has acknowledged his dependence upon the Supreme Being, not only by adoring Him and praying to Him for help, but also by giving back to Him, either directly as a sacrifice, or indirectly as support for religion and the ministers of religion, a portion of the temporal goods which he has received. Thus Cain and Abel offered of their possessions gifts to the Lord.[1] When Noe manifested his gratitude to God, after being saved from the Deluge, by offering a holocaust to Him, God was pleased with the sacrifice and blessed Noe.[2]

In Patriarchical times the obligation of supporting the ministers of God was not so distinct and apparent as it became in later ages. During this early period the father of the family, the Patriarch, was also the priest, the mediator between God and all the members of his family. Naturally, no separate maintenance had to be provided for him, as he was the owner of all the property which the family possessed. As soon, however, as certain persons were recognized as mediators with God, not only for their own immediate family, but also for others, these men received contributions from outside their family. Abraham

[1] *Gen.*, IV, 3-4.
[2] *Gen.*, VIII, 20 et seq.

gave tithes[3] of all that he had recaptured from the kings, who had plundered the Sodomites and the Gomorrhites to Melchisedech, "for he was the priest of the Most High God."[4]

In the Mosaic Dispensation the support of the ministers of religion, and of the various religious activities, was very definitely regulated. The Chosen People were commanded to give the tithes of all the produce of their lands to the Lord as His portion.[5] The right to the use of these tithes God then transferred to the Levites, who were to be His ministers, for their support.[6] The first fruits,[7] offerings promised by vow,[8] and offerings of all other kinds,[9] were also to be given to the Levites for their use.[10] These tithes, first fruits, and various offerings were the principal sources of revenue by means of which the Temple, the service in the Temple, and the ministers were supported throughout the entire period up to the time of Christ.

When Jesus Christ established the New Law, His Church also needed temporal means and accepted them from the faithful. The Gospel accounts show that Christ and His Apostles kept a common purse.[11] As St. John indicates in his Gospel,[12] this purse not only provided for their own daily needs, but also furnished alms for the poor, thus indicating the two chief reasons why the Church has need of material goods, namely, for the support of the Church and her ministers, and for the relief of the temporal wants of the poor and the needy.

As Our Lord and His Apostles were themselves poor, and the latter had even given up their means of livelihood,[13] in order to follow the call of Christ, it may readily be concluded that this common purse was not maintained from

---

[3] *Gen.*, XIV, 20.
[4] *Gen.*, XIV, 18.
[5] *Lev.*, XXVII, 30.
[6] *Num.*, XVIII, 21.
[7] *Num.*, XV, 10-20.
[8] Cf. *Lev.*, XXVII.
[9] Cf. *Lev.*, II-VII, XIV, XV.
[10] *Num.*, XVIII, 8-19.
[11] *Jn.*, XII, 6; *Lk.*, IX, 13; *Mk.*, VI, 37.
[12] *Jn.*, XIII, 29.
[13] *Mt.*, XIX, 27.

their own means, but by the contributions of the other followers of Christ.[14] These people took advantage of this opportunity to help further the Kingdom of God. By relieving Christ and His Apostles from the necessity of supporting themselves by their own labor, they enabled them the better to attend to their spiritual mission.

After the first Pentecost Day, the Christians who lived in and near Jerusalem led a common life with common ownership of all the property they possessed.[15] But as the first fervor passed, dissensions arose,[16] and some of the converts became dissatisfied with the administration and distribution of the property. To free themselves from the cares arising from the management of these goods, the Apostles, that they might the more completely give themselves to prayer and to the preaching of the Word of God, appointed seven deacons,[17] who were to look after the temporal affairs of the community.

This common treasury and community of goods seems, however, to have been unique, and limited to the early congregation of Jerusalem. As the Church spread, the members of the communities that were formed in the various towns and countries kept each their own property, as can be judged from the fact that collections were taken up in various places, at the instance of St. Paul. Thus the congregations of Macedonia and Achaia contributed to help the poor at Jerusalem.[18] St. Paul also ordered the churches of Galatia and Corinth to take up weekly collections for almsgiving.[19]

Throughout the early ages no special provision seems to have been made for the support of the clergy.[20] Many clerics, no doubt, followed the example of St. Paul,[21] and

---

[14] Cf. c. 17, C. XII, q. 1: "Habebat Dominus loculos et a fidelibus oblata conservans et suorum necessitatibus et aliis indigentibus tribuebat."

[15] *Acts*, IV, 34-35.

[16] *Acts*, VI, 1.

[17] *Acts*, VI, 3.

[18] *Rom.*, XV, 26.

[19] I *Cor.*, XVI, 1-2.

[20] Alzog, *Man. of Univ. Church History*, I, 397.

[21] I *Cor.*, II, 12.

rather than be a burden on the faithful, maintained themselves by the work of their own hands.[22] But as the necessity of supporting themselves would tend to distract or even hinder the clergy in the execution of their spiritual functions and duties, the Church looked with disfavor upon the spread of such a custom.[23] She, therefore, frequently passed laws discouraging this practice,[24] limiting the vocations that clerics might engage in,[25] or even forbidding them to follow any secular occupations.[26] And as a general rule the clergy were, as far as this was necessary and possible, always supported by the faithful,[27] who, wishing to fulfill the teaching of Christ [28] that "the laborer is worthy of his hire," willingly contributed to their maintenance.

But even in those places where the clerics supported themselves, money was needed to carry on the activities of the Church. As the representative of Christ, she has always felt herself bound to take special care of His chosen people, the poor and needy; she has constantly tried to give them also temporal and material relief in their wants.[29] And the funds which she needed for this work of charity were in the first centuries obtained in various ways.

The most common way of helping support the Church was for the faithful to bring their free-will offerings when they came to take part in the Holy Sacrifice of the Mass.[30] The bread and the wine which were used in the Holy Sacrifice were the offerings of the faithful.[31] Other articles of food and other necessities, even sums of money, were frequently offered. These, together with the superfluous bread and wine, were intended for the maintenance of the clergy and for the relief of the poor. All of these

---

[22] Alzog, *loc. cit.*

[23] C. Aurelianense (538), can. 11—*Mansi*, IX, 15.

[24] C. Eliberitanum (305), can. 18—*Mansi*, II, 9.

[25] C. Carthag. I (348), can. 6—*Mansi*, III, 147.

[26] Can. Apost. 6: "Episcopus vel presbyter vel diaconus saeculares curas non suscipiat; alioqui deponatur."—*Ante-Nicene Christian Library*, XVII, 259 for English translation.

[27] Alzog, *op. cit.*, I, 658; cf. also Clarke, *History of Tithes*, p. 4.

[28] *Mt.*, X, 19; *Lk.*, X, 7.

[29] Ratzinger, *Geschichte der kirchlichen Armenpflege*, p. VIII.

[30] Bingham, *Antiquities*, bk. V, chap. IV, Sect. I.

[31] *Ibidem.*

offerings were entirely voluntary, as Justin Martyr pointed out:[32] "They that are well-to-do and willing, give what each one thinks fit, and what is collected is deposited with the President, and he succors the orphans and widows." It is interesting to note that at this early time already, when one might expect that those who had the courage to profess the Christian faith, often enough at the risk of their lives during the persecutions, would be generous in the material support of that faith, the same trouble existed which the Church has had to contend with ever since that time. St. Cyprian finds it necessary to reproach some of the faithful, and especially the richer and more powerful, for not bearing their share of the burden of Church support, for not bringing any offerings. On the contrary, as he says, when they come to take part in the celebration of the Sacrifice, they even consume part of that which has been offered up by the poorer members of the community.[33]

Very early also a custom was introduced in various churches of making a special money contribution once a month to the treasury of the church. Tertullian says[34] that this contribution was made "once a month, or when every one pleased...and as they pleased; for no man is compelled to make it, but gives it freely." These monthly donations apparently were used to form a reserve treasury, from which any extraordinary appeals for assistance might be taken care of.[35]

The custom of offering first-fruits, which consisted of a certain small portion of the produce of the individual's property or labor, seems to have been very early and generally introduced. The Apostolical Constitutions[36] contain a very instructive passage, showing to what an extent this custom was applied:

> All the first-fruits of the wine press, the threshing floor, the oxen, and the sheep, shalt thou give to the priest...All the first-fruits of thy hot bread, of thy

---

[32] *Apol.* I, c. 67—*MPG,* VI, 430.

[33] *De Oper. et Eleemos.*—*MPL,* IV, 609.

[34] *Apol.*, c. 39—*MPL,* I, 470.

[35] Cf. Bingham, *Antiquities*, bk. V, ch. IV, Sect. 2.

[36] *Apost. Const.*, VII, 29—*Ante-Nicene Christian Library*, XVII, 189.

> barrels of wine, or oil, or honey, or nuts, or grapes, or the first-fruits of other things, shalt thou give to the priest; but those of silver, and of garments, and of all sort of possessions, to the orphan and to the widow.[37]

Another source of income for the early Church is to be found in the tithes. Since the payment of tithes had been commanded in the Old Testament to the Jews, and was also a very common practice among many pagan peoples,[38] it may be taken for granted that many of the converts, especially those from Judaism, kept on paying these tithes, simply transferring this payment to the Christian community, instead of to the Temple. But, as the giving of tithes was not enforced by any ecclesiastical law, they were rightly regarded as voluntary offerings, pure and simple. The relatively great generosity of most of the Christians [39] precluded the necessity of any special laws, requiring the payment of a fixed amount to the Church. But that tithes were paid, at least in some places, is evident from the fact that the early Christian writers often refer to them in a casual way.[40]

Very early already can also be found the beginnings of what was to be the chief source of revenue for the Church throughout the coming centuries, namely, endowments. At first all immovable property, such as houses and lands, which was donated to the Church, was immediately sold,[41] lest it be confiscated by the State, which looked upon the Church as an illegal society, and, therefore, prohibited from holding property.[42] In time, however, by an ingenious use

---

[37] Regarding the antiquity and the general use of this custom, cf. *Apost. Const.*, II, 35 and VIII, 30—*Ante-Nicene Christian Library*, XVII, 65 and 243; *Apost. Canons*, can. 5—*op. cit.*, p. 258; *Origen contra Cels.*, VIII—*MPG*, XI, 1522 et seq.; Irenaeus (+196), IV, 32 and 34—*MPG*, VII, 1070 et seq. and 1083 et seq.; Nazianzen, Ep. 80—*MPG*, XXXVI, 154.

[38] Cf. William Fanning, "Tithes," *Cath. Ency.*, XIV, 741-742.

[39] Gasquet, *Parish Life in Medieval England*, p. 10.

[40] Cf. *Apost. Const.*, VII, 29 and VIII, 30—*Ante-Nicene Christian Library*, XVII, 189 and 243; also Clarke, *Hist. of Tithes*, p. XVIII, where he says that tithes are mentioned in some of the episcopal writings of the 2nd and 3d centuries.

[41] Cf. Bingham, *Antiquities*, bk. V, ch. IV, Sect. 5.

[42] Vogt., *Kirchliches Vermögensrecht*, p. 3.

of the state law, various Christian communities formed funeral colleges,[43] and as such were recognized by the State, and could legally acquire and hold property.[44] It is impossible to determine just when this practice began, but that it antedated the year 200 can be concluded from the fact that Tertullian speaks about it as being an actual fact in his *Apologeticus,* which was written about the year 197.

The first legal acknowledgment of this practice is found during the reign of the Emperor Alexander Severus (222–235).

> A piece of ground in Rome, which was litigated by a company of victuallers, was awarded by the Emperor (Alexander Severus) himself to the Christians, upon the principle that it was better that it should be devoted to the worship of God in any form than applied to a profane and unworthy use.[45]

After this time references to the property of the Church can be found in various enactments of the Emperors.[46] But that such endowments ever became very extensive, before the time of Constantine, is hardly credible, since they were in constant danger of confiscation, and actually were confiscated on various occasions.[47] As a general rule, the Christians were too prudent to hold too much property in this way, subject to the whims of hostile Emperors, who, as absolute rulers, could at any time, by a simple decree, confiscate it all.

These, then, were the chief methods of support practiced in the early Church: donations, usually of food, at the occasion of the Sacrifice of the Mass; monthly donations of money to the Church treasury; first-fruits; tithes, to some extent; and legacies or donations of lands and houses, which were either sold immediately and the proceeds used, or else held as an endowment by the Christian community to

---

[43] Tertullian, *Apol.,* c. 39—*MPL,* I, 470.

[44] Vogt, *op. cit.,* p. 3.

[45] Milman, *History of Christianity,* II, 183; based on a passage from Aelius Lampridius. Cf. also Funk, *Lehrbuch der Kirchengeschichte,* I, 67.

[46] Milman, *op. cit.,* II, 195, 220-1; cf. also Lactantius, *De mortibus persecutorum,* c. 48—*MPL,* VII, 267.

[47] Milman, *op. cit.,* II, 195, 220-1.

which this property had been given. Everything that the Church received was given voluntarily, as there was no legal or physical compulsion. That moral suasion or even moral compulsion was sometimes resorted to, can easily enough be inferred by one who has had some experience of their occasional need in the Church in this country, as also from certain passages in the writings of the early Christians.[48]

Whether or not the income of the Church was adequate cannot be determined. No doubt she could make good use of all that was donated. The recipients of her charity must have been many. Most of the wealth, especially in the cities, where the first Christian communities were founded,[49] was in the hands of a few. The proportionate number of poor people being so enormously great, many of these must have found themselves in absolute want. Besides this, most of her members belonged to the poorer class, since they were most eager and willing to receive the message of hope in another and better life, that the Church offered. In such a condition of society, even the exceptional generosity of those of her members who were able to help,[50] would hardly permit her to provide for any but the most urgent needs. The generous aid, which she was to receive from the State during the coming centuries, must, therefore, have proven very welcome.

2.—From the Edict of Milan to the Re-establishment of the Roman Empire (313–800)

The accession of Constantine to the Imperial dignity marked a turning-point in the history of the Church. Inspired by a supernatural vision, Constantine had placed his army and his cause under the protection of the God of the

---

[48] E.g., cf. St. Cyprian, *De Oper. et Eleemos.—MPL*, IV, 609, passages of which could very easily be confused with quotations from the announcements of some present-day pastor, who, because of the indifference of his flock, finds himself laboring under serious financial difficulties.

[49] Funk, *Lehrbuch der Kirchengeschichte*, I, 49.

[50] Cf. Gasquet, *Parish Life in Medieval England*, p. 10.

Christians,[51] and in the decisive battle at the Milvian Bridge, on October 28th, 312, routed the forces of his predecessor, the Emperor Maxentius.

The new Emperor now showed his gratitude to the Christian God by issuing his renowned Edict of Toleration, at Milan, in February, 313. By this Edict freedom of worship was extended to all. The Christian religion, in particular, was granted all the rights and privileges which the pagan state religions had enjoyed. The decree also ordered that all the private and communal property, which had been confiscated during the time of the persecutions, should be restored to the Christians.[52] The Christian Church was recognized as a legal society, with full powers to acquire and hold property.[53]

Under such favorable conditions, the Church flourished and the numbers of the faithful increased rapidly.[54] In 321, Constantine passed a law permitting everybody to bequeath whatever part of his property he pleased to the Church.[55] As a result of the liberality of the faithful, who vied with each other in their donations and bequests, great additions were made to the endowments and to the standing revenues of the churches.[56] Many members of the rich nobility, who had joined the Church, offered magnificent examples to the rest of the faithful by their large donations, some even assigning the whole of their enormous estates to pious causes.[57] Thus, in 404, Pinianus and his wife, St. Melania, consecrated their entire fortune, consisting of valuable property in Rome itself and over 60 farms and 400 slaves, to the Church and to the poor.[58] Sts. Marcella and Paula, two noble ladies, disposed of their large fortunes in a like manner,[59] as also the Senator Pammachius,[60] Lea, a rich

51 Eusebius, *Vit. Const.*, bk. I, ch. XX—*MPG*, XX, 943.
52 Eusebius, *Hist. Eccl.*, bk. X, ch. V—*MPG*, XX, 882-3.
53 Vogt, *Kirchliches Vermögensrecht*, p. 3.
54 Sozomen, *Eccl. Hist.*, bk. I, ch. VI—*MPG*, LXVII, 871.
55 *Cod. Just.*, I, 2. 1.
56 Bingham, *Antiquities*, bk. V, ch. IV, Sect. 5.
57 Grisar, *Rome and the Popes*, I, 44.
58 Funk, *Lehrbuch der Kirchengeschichte*, I, 296.
59 Grisar, *op. cit.*, I, 58-59.
60 *Ibidem*, p. 54.

widow, and Fabiola, a daughter of the ancient Fabian family.[61] Of the Princess Pulcheria, the virgin sister of Theodosius the Younger, Sozomen says:[62] "It would take a long time to describe the magnificent houses of prayer which she erected, the hospitals for the relief of the poor and of strangers which she founded, and the monastical institutions which she endowed." The middle classes and the poor, emulating such generosity, were in proportion equally liberal.[63]

Another source of considerable help in the support of the Church, which was developed during this period, consisted in the system of patronage.[64] Laics, who built and endowed churches, were granted certain privileges regarding the appointment of the clergy who were attached to these churches.[65] The granting of such privileges by the Church, as a mark of gratitude to these generous benefactors, no doubt, also served as an incentive to others to make similar donations. That they actually were numerous may be adduced from the fact that both the Church [66] and the State [67] found it expedient to pass laws regulating the right of patronage.

The regular paying of the tithes was also urged upon the faithful. "As the Church grew, its needs, and in particular, the less obvious needs of the faithful poor, required some more regular and certain resources than the irregular and voluntary alms of its richer members." [68] The system of tithes, finding its sanction in the divine ordinance of the Old Testament,[69] would naturally offer the most certain method of assuring such a regular income. That tithes were demanded of the faithful, possibly already in the fourth century,[70] is evident from the enactments of the

---

[61] *Ibidem,* p. 60.

[62] *Eccl. Hist.,* bk. X, ch. I—*MPG,* LXVII, 1595.

[63] Sozomen, *Eccl. Hist.,* bk. III, ch. XVIII—*MPG,* LXVII, 1095.

[64] Godfrey, *The Right of Patronage,* p. 39.

[65] *Ibidem,* p. 21.

[66] C. 31, C. XVI, q. 1; also c. 4, XVIII, q. 2.

[67] *Nov.,* 57, c. 2; also *Nov.,* 123, c. 18.

[68] Gasquet, *Parish Life in Medieval England,* pp. 10-11.

[69] *Num.,* XXVII, 30-34.

[70] Bingham, *Antiquities,* bk. V, ch. V, Sect. 3.

Council of Macon, which was held in 585. The Fathers of this Council commanded the faithful to re-establish the "old custom" of paying tithes, of fulfilling this duty which "the whole of Christendom, for a long time, had observed inviolate." [71] They stress the fact that they are not laying a new obligation upon the faithful, but are merely reasserting an old established and admitted Christian principle, which, in the course of time, had fallen into neglect.[72]

Another stable source of income for the Church was the allowance which the State made to the clergy. Constantine and his successors, looking upon the Church as the bulwark of the State, rightly felt that it was to their advantage, and the duty of the State, to strengthen this defense by aiding it with generous grants from the State funds. In 324, therefore, Constantine repaired those churches "which were of sufficient magnitude, enlarged and beautified others, and erected new edifices in places in which no building...had existed previously." [73] In 325 he "erected magnificent temples to God in every place, particularly in metropolises, such as Nicomedia, Antioch, and Byzantium." [74] As the occasion required, he also made large payments to the clergy of various churches for their maintenance.[75] On one occasion he ordered 3000 polles [76] to be given to the Bishop of Carthage, to be distributed among his clergy for their present necessities.[77] He also wrote to the governors of the provinces, ordering that a fixed allowance should be given every year "in every city to orphans and widows, and to those who were consecrated to the divine service." [78] Julian withdrew this allowance, but his successors ordered

---

[71] C. Matisconense II (585), c. 5—*Mansi,* IX, 952: "Unde statuimus . . . ut mos antiquus a fidelibus reparetur . . . Quas leges Christianorum congeries longis temporibus custodivit intemeratas . . ."

[72] *Ibidem.*

[73] Sozomen, *Eccl. Hist.,* bk. I, ch. VIII—*MPG,* LXVII, 875 et seq.

[74] Sozomen, *op. cit.,* bk. II, ch. III—*MPG,* LXVII, 935.

[75] Bingham, *Antiquities,* bk. V, ch. IV, Sect. 7.

[76] Cf. Babelon, *Traité des Monnaies,* etc., vol. I, Part I, 762 et seq., on the value of the "folles," as it was also called. 3000 polles was equivalent to about 19,500 grains of gold, about $850, a large sum of money at that time.

[77] Eusebius, *Hist. Eccl.,* bk. X, ch. VI—*MPG,* XX, 891.

[78] Theodoret, *Eccl. Hist.,* bk. I, ch. X—*MPG,* LXXXII, 938.

that it be again paid.[79] Owing, however, to the diminished income of the State, they saw themselves compelled to limit it to the third part of the original allowance, which still formed a very respectable sum.[80] Different emperors also gave a number of heathen temples to the Church, and the revenues of the lands belonging to these temples were settled upon the clergy.[81]

In reviewing this period, one finds, as its salient development in Church maintenance, the widespread establishment of founded benefices, or endowments. Large donations of lands or houses were kept by the Church, the revenues thereof being expended for her needs. These endowments were continually increased by the gifts of the faithful, until some churches found themselves in the possession of very large estates.[82] Thus the property of the Roman See, the Patrimony of Peter, as it was called, had, by the time of Gregory the Great (590–604), increased to such an extent that the Holy See was able to exert a decided political influence.[83] Other churches, and in particular the Metropolitan Sees, were endowed in like proportion. The administration of these ecclesiastical properties became so important that many councils considered it necessary to pass laws regulating this administration.[84] And so general was the custom of endowing churches, and so commonly was it looked upon as the one principal source of support for these churches, that statutes were in force, in various countries, forbidding the dedication of a church until it had an endowment sufficient to take care of all the ordinary expenses of the church.[85]

---

[79] *Ibidem.*

[80] *Ibidem.*

[81] E.g., Emperor Honorius; cf. *Cod. Theod.*, XVI, 10. 20.

[82] Alzog, *Man. of Univ. Ch. Hist.*, II, 130.

[83] Funk, *Lehrbuch der Kirchengeschichte*, I, 362-363. Regarding the Papal estates and their size, cf. Creighton, *History of the Popes during the Reformation*, I, 7.

[84] Among others, C. Toletanum (597), c. 2—*Mansi*, X, 477; C. Emeritense (666), c. 19—*Mansi*, XI, 85; C. Toletanum (693), c. 5—*Mansi*, XII, 72.

[85] E.g., C. Bracarense, III (572), c. 5—*Mansi*, IX, 839.

And yet, in spite of all this support, in spite of the fact that the Church tried to provide itself with a stable and adequate income by the establishment of revenue yielding foundations, by the regulation of the tithes, by obtaining the financial support of the State, and by urging the faithful to be as generous as possible in their voluntary contributions; as time went on, the clergy, the monasteries and the charitable institutions of all kinds were often in great need of assistance.[86] The reason for these conditions is to be found in the social upheavals which occurred during the second half of this period. The Roman State and Roman society had been weighed in the balance of the Judgment of God and had been found wanting. For four long centuries the Gospel of Christ had been preached to the people; again and again had the prophets of God warned it of the coming destruction.[87] "It is in consequence of our sins that the Barbarians gain the upper hand—on account of our vices that the Roman armies are defeated," St. Jerome had cried out.[88] But so corrupt, so steeped in the old heathen vices and immorality was the public and social life of the Empire,[89] that the Providence of God, through the barbarian invasions, finally swept it off the boards of the world, to make room for a new Roman Empire, the Holy Roman Empire of Charlemagne and his successors, the Empire founded on the convert children of the pagan barbarians who had destroyed the old Empire with all its deep-rooted heathen customs and traditions.

During these migrations of nations, these upheavals and disasters, so cataclysmic and far-reaching that many looked upon them as signs of the coming dissolution of the world,[90] the Church lost practically all of those rich treasures with which the piety of her children had endowed her.[91] During

---

[86] Alzog, *Man. of Univ. Ch. Hist.*, II, 131; also Link, *Mess-Stipendien*, p. 85.

[87] Cf. St. Ambrose, *De ieiunio*, c. 12, 18, 22, 23—*MPL*, XIV, 711 et seq.; St. Jerome, *Ep.* 22 and 125—*MPL*, XXII, 394 and 1072 respectively; Salvianus, *De Gubernatione Dei*—*MPL*, LIII, 128 et seq.

[88] *Ep.* 60, *ad Heliodorum*, no. 17—*MPL*, XXII, 601.

[89] Cf. Grisar, *Rome and the Popes*, I, 47 et seq.

[90] Grisar, *op. cit.*, III, 185.

[91] Grisar, *op. cit.*, III, 177-184; also Link, *Mess-Stipendien*, p. 84.

the continual wars and invasions marauding armies overran entire countries. Not only were the churches despoiled of everything valuable that could either be carried away or destroyed, even her sources of revenue were lost by the impoverishment of the peoples. The little that was left to her she gladly and freely spent to alleviate the universal misery. The Church had always claimed that all her property was the property of the poor.[92] She now proved the sincerity of her claims by sacrificing everything, if necessary, even selling the sacred vessels,[93] and using the proceeds to feed and clothe the needy and ransom the captives. The close of this period found her almost as poor as she had been at the beginning.[94]

3.—From Charlemagne to the Council of Trent (800–1500)

The outstanding characteristic in Church support during the period extending from the coronation of Charlemagne to the Council of Trent is the increase in the number and in the value of the endowments. The endowment system of supporting churches and religious institutions was looked upon with favor, both by the clergy and the laity, as it provided a certain and permanent income. It was the wish of the Church, therefore, that all parishes and religious institutions should acquire endowments whose revenues should be sufficient to cover their ordinary expenses.[95]

As has already been mentioned, the endowment system traces its origin back to the ages of persecution. After the time of Constantine it became very prevalent throughout the Roman Empire. Most of these earlier foundations were, however, lost in the centuries of turmoil that followed. During these warlike ages even Christian princes

---

[92] St. Augustine, *Ep.* 185 *ad Bonifac.—MPL*, XXXIII, 809: "Non sunt illa nostra, sed pauperum quorum procurationem quodammodo gerimus, non proprietatem nobis usurpatione damnabili vindicamus." St. Ambrose, *Ep.* 18 *ad Valent.—MPL*, XVI, 977: "Nihil ecclesia sibi nisi fidem possidet . . . possessio ecclesiae est sumptus egenorum."

[93] Ratzinger, *Geschichte der Armenpflege*, p. 119.

[94] Grisar, *op. cit.*, I, 82-85.

[95] C. Bracarense, III (572), c. 5—*Mansi*, IX, 839; also c. 1, X, *De Censibus, Exactionibus et Procurationibus*, III, 39.

did not hesitate to seize Church property for their own purposes. Thus, Charles Martel (714-741), finding it impossible to pay his soldiers from the State treasury, suppressed diocesan and monastic foundations, confiscated their properties, and used these to obtain the necessary funds.[96] The revenues of other benefices, which he did not suppress, he bestowed upon State officials.[97] His son, Pepin, employed the same means to refill the state coffers.[98] Even Charlemagne, during the first decade of his rule, frequently resorted to a secularization of Church properties.[99] But with the return of stable conditions in society, and with the increasing conformity of all thought and action to Christian ideals, the property of the Church came to be considered the property of God, so sacred and inviolable that, during the next centuries, the ages of faith, few indeed were rash and impious enough to take any of it for their own use.

By far the greater number of these foundations owed their origin to the munificence of some king, noble, or rich landowner. These would erect a church, a monastery or a charitable institution, and endow it with sufficient property, usually in the form of land, to enable it to subsist.[100] But "property in greater or lesser amounts, houses, lands, cattle, and rich hangings, etc., was constantly being left by will, or otherwise given" [101] to these institutions, so that in the course of time, the foundations increased considerably. Especially numerous were such donations during the time of the Crusades. Many of the crusaders, feeling certain that they would lose their lives in the holy wars, wished to make their sacrifice complete, and, therefore, before leaving, made over their entire property to the Church. Others, who expected to settle down in Palestine, disposed of their

---

96 Funk, *Lehrbuch der Kirchengeschichte,* I, 399-400.

97 Funk, *op. cit.*, I, 399-400.

98 Alzog, *Man. of Univ. Ch. Hist.*, II, 130-132.

99 Funk, *op. cit.*, I, 399-400.

100 For examples, cf. Hope, *St. Boniface and the Conversion of Germany,* I, 47, 61, 73, 92, 111, 158, et al.; Barrett, "The Pre-Reformation Church in Scotland," *The Amer. Cath. Quart. Rev.*, XXIII (1898), 786; Alzog, *Man. of Univ. Ch. Hist.*, II, 247-248, 232; Clarke, *History of Tithes,* p. 24.

101 Gasquet, *Parish Life in Medieval England,* p. 110.

property at home for very nominal prices, the Church often being the beneficiary.[102]

In the course of time the holdings of many churches and monasteries became enormous, due to the fact that the Church considered all these donations and bequests pious trusts which were not to be alienated.[103] Thus, during the fourteenth century the Archbishop of Prague ruled over 329 towns and villages, which were situated in the territories belonging to that See, and over 300 ecclesiastics were maintained from the revenues of the cathedral.[104] The lands belonging to the Sees of Mentz, Cologne, and Treves were so extensive that the prelates of these Sees were ranked with the princes and electors of the German Empire. In 1803, when the estates of these three Sees, and those of fourteen others, were secularized, it was computed that an annual revenue of $8,410,400 was lost to the Church.[105]

Many monasteries also became very wealthy. During the fifteenth century the yearly revenues of the religious houses in County Meath, in Ireland, amounted to about $337,500; in Kildare County, $95,625; in Louth County, $225,000; and in Dublin County, $337,500,[106] very respectable sums, indeed, for those times. In the sixteenth century the Abbey of Abroath, in Scotland, "could boast of an annual revenue equivalent to $50,000 of our money."[107] Many other instances could be cited to show how rich the Church became during these ages of faith, due to the generosity of the faithful.

But this very generosity often threatened to defeat its own purpose. Lands and territories donated to the Church became so great that the bishops and abbots, being lords of these considerable territories, were forced to govern them as civil rulers. They were at the heads of the civil governments, often the most powerful in the land; they had to

---

[102] Alzog., *Manual of Univ. Ch. Hist.*, II, 650.

[103] C. 19, C. XII, q. 2.

[104] Creighton, *Hist. of the Papacy during the Reformation*, I, 308.

[105] Alzog, *Man. of Univ. Ch. Hist.*, III, 676-677.

[106] MacCaffrey, *Hist. of the Cath. Ch. from the Renaissance to the Reformation*, II, 264.

[107] Barrett, "The Pre-Reformation Church in Scotland," in the *Am. Cath. Quart. Rev.*, XXIII (1898), 786.

assist in the business of the state of which their territories formed a part; they had to maintain a corps of troops in the service of their sovereigns; above all, they had to maintain a large body of civil officials to help govern their territories. The result was a tendency towards secularization; the Church properties and livings were more and more being utilized to maintain these armies and lay officials, rather than to serve as a support for the Church and the clergy.[108]

To counteract this increasing employment of Church revenues for secular purposes, another tendency necessarily made itself felt. The revenues of certain defined portions of these estates were set aside for the upkeep of the cathedral church and the clergy connected with it, or of the monastery and its members. The remaining income was left at the disposal of the bishop or abbot, to be used for his support, as the civil ruler, and for the support of the civil government, which he conducted.[109]

The Church had to struggle unceasingly to vindicate to herself at least a portion of these revenues, all of which had been intended for her use and for the relief of the needy. This proved to be the case especially then when these positions of wealth and power, the episcopal and abbatial offices, were occupied by men who had entered the clerical state, not because of any supernatural motive, but because they expected to become powerful by attaining these offices. These men not only squandered the possessions of the Church in the furtherance of their own ambitions and pleasures, but were a continual source of scandal and disaffection to all the faithful.

Besides these endowments, the Church possessed another source of very considerable revenues in the tithes. Tithes, indeed, had been paid in earlier times, ever since the establishment of the Church. The payment of these tithes had, however, never become a general practice. During the preceding centuries they had been introduced and their payment enforced in various places, generally, however, with

---

[108] Cf. Pöschl, *Bischofsgut und Mensa Episcopalis*, I, 2-3, regarding this development.

[109] *Ibidem*, pp. 3-5.

but indifferent success.[110] Now, however, the State promulgated and enforced laws commanding the payment of these tithes to the Church. In 779, Charlemagne, to indemnify the Church for the secularizations which he had effected, introduced the tithes throughout the Frankish Kingdom.[111] In England, where the payment of tithes had acquired the force of century-old custom, it was also made legally binding in 927 by a law of King Athelstan.[112] Other countries passed similar laws, so that, about this time, the legal enforcement of the duty of paying the tithes became general throughout Christianity.[113]

In the beginning the tithes were exacted only from the fruits of the fields, but they were gradually extended to other products, so that they finally were imposed upon every branch of industry.[114] Speaking about the tithes in England, Wall observes: "In the thirteenth century it was ordained that the tithes of all fisheries...be paid entire... The tithe of young animals was to be paid," as also "of the fruits of the field...Tithe is also to be paid of cheese, milk, bees, wood, meadows, waters, mills, warrens, fisheries, osiers, gardens, and the profit of trade." [115] The duty of paying tithes of all income, whether it be from the fields or from any other possible sources, had been enforced even earlier on the Continent.[116]

Voluntary contributions of all kinds also helped to increase the revenues of the Church. These contributions, since they were dependent on the piety and the prosperity of the individual Christians, always remained an uncertain quantity in the income of the Church. Various contributions, however, became customary in different localities, and could be relied on as a stable factor. A brief description and enumeration of some of the ways in which voluntary contributions were gathered in the English Church,

---

110 Funk, *Lehrbuch der Kirchengeschichte*, I, 400.

111 *Ibidem.*

112 Clarke, *History of Tithes*, p. 70.

113 Funk, *op. cit.*, I, 400.

114 *Ibidem.*

115 Wall, J. Charles, *An Old English Parish*, pp. 60-61.

116 Alzog, *Man. of Univ. Ch. Hist.*, II, 355.

may serve as a norm for the systems of voluntary contributions that were practiced in other countries of Christian Europe.

Stole fees, offerings made for various services rendered to individuals, such as baptism, marriage, churching of women, funerals, etc., were customarily paid.[117] These fees ordinarily belonged to the minister who rendered these services, as did also the stipend for the Mass, an offering made for a Mass to be said or sung for a particular person or intention. A certain regular oblation, to be made every Sunday and Feastday, to him who had the care of souls, became customary in many places.[118] This payment was usually made to the pastor, and became so customary that, in many places, its payment could be enforced by law.[119]

Other methods "by which the people of a parish raised money for their works were many and various, and some of them curious." [120] Thus there was the voluntary assessment which was proportioned to the wealth of the individual parishioners,[121] and the joint voluntary gifts made by several people for some special purpose, such as the buying of vestments, bells, etc.[122] Collections were also taken up at various times and in various ways. Boys went from house to house, several times a year, with collecting bags; men carried holy pictures or relics around to arouse the devotion and generosity of the people; various brotherhoods or guilds went about the parish to collect, carrying their corporation banners or the parish cross; collection-boxes were set up in the vestibules of the churches to raise funds for particular purposes.[123] Special fees were also paid on the occasions of marriages or funerals, for the use of various articles belonging to the church, such as the "best cross" in funeral processions.[124] Parishioners, over fourteen years of age, were exhorted to make special offerings four times

---

[117] Gasquet, *Parish Life in Medieval England*, p. 86.
[118] Gasquet, *op. cit.*, p. 87.
[119] *Ibidem.*
[120] Gasquet, *op. cit.*, p. 124.
[121] *Ibidem.*
[122] Gasquet, *op. cit.*, pp. 125-126.
[123] Gasquet, *op. cit.*, pp. 127-128.
[124] Gasquet, *op. cit.*, p. 132.

a year, at Christmas, Easter, and the Patronal and Dedication Feasts; to subscribe Church-scot for church expenses, at Martin-mas; Light-scot for illuminating the church; plough-alms in spring; and Peter's Pence on St. Peter's Day.[125]

Another profitable source of revenue were the festive entertainments, called church ales, which "have almost their exact counterparts in our modern public dinners for charitable purposes." [126] Generous parishioners would provide the food and ale. "The inevitable collection followed; and, according to the goodness of the feast, the number of the guests, or their satisfaction with the arrangements made, the amount of donations was large or small." [127] The women of the parish would also hold dancing parties at certain times, to help raise funds for some special purpose.[128] "Hock-day," a festival commemorating the annihilation of the Danes in 1002, was also very generally celebrated with certain traditional customs, and the ever recurring plea to contribute to the collection would be made.[129] In some places the parish even entered into the field of business, taking over the baking of the bread for the entire parish, and also the brewing and sale of ale.[130]

By means of all these sources, the endowment revenues, the tithes, the contributions and bequests, and the numerous and often ingeniously evolved special collections, the income of the Church was generally very great during these ages. As long as this wealth was used for the purposes for which it was given, the support of the clergy, of the Church activities and buildings, and the relief of the poor, the faithful did not begrudge it to the Church. People have always been especially willing to enrich an institution which distributed the proceeds of its wealth with an open hand to the poor. That the Church was faithful to this trust is shown by the fact that State support of the poor

---

[125] Wall, *An Old English Parish*, p. 63.

[126] Gasquet, *op. cit.*, p. 239, quoting Dr. Jessop.

[127] *Ibidem.*

[128] Gasquet, *op. cit.*, p. 243.

[129] Gasquet, *op. cit.*, p. 241.

[130] Gasquet, *op. cit.*, p. 243.

and aged was practically unknown during these ages when the Church had the means to provide for this need.

The monasteries especially were always looked upon as the unfailing support of everybody in distress. And if these monasteries stored up treasure during the times of prosperity, the faithful knew that they would be willing to expend it for charity whenever it was necessary. On one occasion, during a time of famine, "no less than four thousand were, for three months, daily fed by the loving charity of the monks" of Melrose Abbey, in Scotland.[131] The obligation of charity was so well understood by the religious orders that the "almonry gate," as it was called in England, was an established institution in practically all monasteries. This was the gate at which food was daily distributed to all who came and asked. The possessions of the Church may be regarded as the savings banks of the Middle Ages. When the faithful were prosperous they were very generous in their contributions to the Church, knowing that, if times of famine or need should come, the Church will be willing to expend all these riches in charity.

4.—After the Council of Trent, Outside of the United States

The period of transition from the Middle Ages to modern times ushered in the great disruption of the Church, commonly known as the "Protestant Reformation." Rumors of the coming trouble began to make themselves heard in the latter part of the preceding period. Only too frequently had the people been scandalized and alienated from the Church by the various abuses which, in different places, had crept into her government and discipline. Many of these abuses arose because of the material wealth of the Church. When the faithful saw that the revenues from the endowments and the tithes, instead of being employed for the purposes of charity and religion, were all too often appropriated by laymen for their own use, sometimes through the connivance of some unscrupulous person who had managed to insinuate himself into the hierarchy of the

[131] Barrett, "The Pre-Reformation Church in Scotland," in the *Am. Cath. Quart. Rev.*, XXIII (1898), 797.

Church, their generosity quickly decreased.[132] And when these unscrupulous prelates resorted to extortion to enrich themselves,[133] the oppressed people included the entire Church in their resentment against such injustice.

Under these conditions, agitators found it an easy matter to convert these people to their specious doctrines; that the Church and her ministers should not own any property,[134] and that, therefore, all material support should be denied to the Church. The temporal rulers, impoverished by the frequent wars, also listened with favor to the natural deduction which was drawn from this doctrine, that the State could and should confiscate all Church properties.[135] Although these teachings were condemned and suppressed,[136] the avarice of the temporal princes and the resentment of the common people kept them alive until they brought forth their logical fruit, the heresy of Protestantism.[137]

When the break did come and entire communities, even states, fell away from their allegiance to the Church, the rulers of these states immediately suppressed the monasteries, the charitable institutions and diocesan foundations, and confiscated their possessions.[138] The parochial endowments followed the parishes to which they were attached over into the new religious field.[139] In this way all the foundations which the Church had gradually accumulated during the preceding centuries in northern Germany,[140] in the Scandinavian countries,[141] in Holland,[142] in England,[143]

---

[132] Doheny, *Church Property, Modes of Acquisition*, p. 11.

[133] *Ibidem.*

[134] Funk, *Lehrbuch der Kirchengeschichte*, II, 610.

[135] Doheny, *op. cit.*, p. 12.

[136] Joannes, XXII, const., *Cum inter nonnullos*, 13 Nov., 1323—Denzinger-Bannwart, *Enchiridion*, n. 494-500; Joannes XXII, const., *Licet*, 23 Oct., 1327—*Fontes*, n. 38; Martinus V, const., *Inter cunctas*, 22 Febr., 1418—*Fontes*, n. 43.

[137] Funk, *op. cit.*, II, 609-612.

[138] Funk, *Lehrbuch der Kirchengeschichte*, II, 707 and 709.

[139] Vogt, *Kirchliches Vermögensrecht*, p. 41.

[140] Funk, *Lehrbuch der Kirchengeschichte*, II, 743.

[141] Funk, *op. cit.*, II, 746-747.

[142] Funk, *op. cit.*, II, 770.

[143] Funk, *op. cit.*, II, 751-752.

and Scotland [144] were lost. In Ireland, where the people signalized themselves by their gallant adherence to the Catholic faith, during the centuries of persecution to which they were subjected, the property of their churches was also confiscated by the English government, the parochial benefices to be handed over to the Anglican ministers, and the monasteries and other institutions, with their lands, sold for the benefit of the State and its officials.[145]

In the Catholic countries of Southern Europe, i.e., in Southern Germany, France, the Austrian lands, Italy, Spain and Portugal, the Catholic religion remained the State religion, and her possessions were protected by the State. Except for occasional and partial secularizations, brought about by the spread of liberalistic teachings, most of her property was kept intact until the middle of the eighteenth century.

France was the first of these countries to begin the attack upon the Church. Even before the Revolution the enemies of the Church were trying to destroy her. They reasoned that the most effective way to attain their purpose was to destroy, first of all, her strongest support, the religious orders. The attack was, therefore, begun in 1745, by inducing the Government to subscribe to a plan for the gradual abolition of the religious houses.[146] In the beginning only the smaller communities were suppressed,[147] the suspicions of the Catholic people being allayed with some trumped-up reasons of expediency and economy. The movement grew, as these men became bolder, and in 1762 the 84 colleges conducted by the Jesuits in France were closed and their endowments confiscated.[148] Then the storm broke forth in the French Revolution, and in 1789–90, all religious houses, with a few exceptions, were suppressed and their property confiscated; [149] the tithes, which had yielded the Church an

---

[144] Funk, *op. cit.*, II, 759-760.

[145] Alzog, *Man. of Univ. Ch. Hist.*, III, 728-729.

[146] Sampson, "Pius VI and the French Revolution," *Am. Cath. Quart. Rev.*, XXXI (1906), 221.

[147] *Ibidem.*

[148] Sampson, *op. cit.*, p. 222.

[149] Alzog, *Man. of Univ. Ch. Hist.*, III, 636-637.

annual income of seventy million francs, were abolished;[150] and all ecclesiastical property confiscated by the government.[151] The State agreed to support the clergy from the State treasury, but this promise was quickly forgotten.[152]

In the Concordat of 1801, Napoleon obtained a condonation of all these secularizations from the Holy See,[153] and in return promised to pay a specified salary to the clergy as an indemnity for the stolen property.[154] This salary was paid by the French Governments with reasonable regularity until the Law of Separation was passed in 1905.[155] During this century of comparative peace the generosity of the faithful had again endowed the ecclesiastical institutions to such an extent that these endowments yielded an annual income of over ninety million dollars. This, together with the eight million, which the Church received each year from the State, assured her a steady and permanent income of about one hundred million dollars, not considering the contributions of the people.[156]

All this was lost when the "Law of Separation" went into effect. Not only was the State support withdrawn, but all the property of the Church, even the church edifices and the parochial residences, was confiscated. The only concession made was that parishes, upon application, were granted the use of the parish churches and rectories, if they agreed to maintain them.[157] Since then the Church has relied entirely upon the contributions of the faithful for her support. As the people, however, were not accustomed to contribute in such a way and in such amounts as to provide a steady and sufficient income, the Church found herself at first considerably embarrassed in her activities.[158] Various methods were tried by the episcopate to raise the necessary funds. In

---

150 Alzog, *op. cit.*, III, 634-635.

151 Alzog, *op. cit.*, III, 636.

152 *Ibidem.*

153 Vogt, *Kirchliches Vermögensrecht*, p. 43.

154 Funk, *Lehrbuch der Kirchengeschichte*, II, 890.

155 *Ibidem.*

156 Boyd, "The French Ecclesiastical Revolution," *Am. Cath. Quart. Rev.*, XXXII (1907), 648.

157 Parsons, "Separation of Church and State in France," *Am. Cath. Quart. Rev.*, XXXI (1906), 509-510.

158 Platz, *Geistige Kämpfe im modernen Frankreich*, p. 491.

some dioceses, parochial associations were formed by the men and women who were anxious to secure the continuance of the Church services. In other places, wealthy families took upon themselves the entire burden of the support of their parish churches. In numerous districts, however, aggregating about one-third of entire France, religious indifference had become so prevalent that the clergy were unable to raise more than a small fraction of the amount necessary for their own sustenance, not to speak of other expenses such as the erection and maintenance of parochial schools.[159]

To enable the Church to continue her work in these districts, the bishops decided to establish an interdiocesan fund by a contribution from each diocese of five per cent of its income. From this fund the poorer dioceses were to receive supplementary grants, as the need might arise.[160] So satisfactory has this arrangement proven that not only has the Church been able to maintain its worship but has even succeeded in raising sufficient funds for the establishment of Catholic schools all over France, in order to preserve her youth from the contaminating influence of the anti-Catholic, state supported schools.[161] Far from destroying the French Church, this persecution has been the occasion of a reawakening of faith, a revival of respect for the clergy, and the return of many, who had become indifferent, their religious duties.[162]

The middle of the 18th century also marked the opening of a period of persecution and of confiscations of ecclesiastical possessions in the Italian States. In 1764, in the territory of Parma-Piacenza, the Church's right to receive inheritances and bequests was limited;[163] in 1769–70, the

---

[159] Dimnet, "The Church in France, Its Present Position," in the *Dublin Review*, XXXI (1906), 178.

[160] Boyd, "The French Ecclesiastical Revolution," in the *Am. Cath. Quart. Rev.*, XXXII (1907), 642.

[161] Gwynn, "For the Good Name of France," *The Commonweal*, IX (1929), 384.

[162] Boyd, "The French Ecclesiastical Revolution," in the *Am. Cath. Quart. Rev.*, XXXII (1907), 648.

[163] Sampson, "Pius VI and the French Revolution," in the *Am. Cath. Quart. Rev.*, XXXI (1906), 229.

Neapolitan government abolished the payment of tithes, seized the revenues of various benefices, and suppressed numerous monasteries, confiscating their possessions.[164] Venice also passed laws limiting the value of the donations and bequests which could be made to the Church, and also confiscated the properties of a number of monasteries.[165] During the French Revolution the Holy See lost its territories in France, whilst the French invasions, which occurred at that time, resulted in great material losses for the Church throughout Italy.[166]

King Victor Emmanuel of Piedmont reopened the attack on the Church in 1848 by the suppression of the Jesuits living in his territories. This was followed by the abolition of the tithes in 1850 and the suppression and confiscation of property of almost all the religious houses in 1855.[167] As he gradually brought the other states of Italy under his sway, the same measures were carried out in these lands, together with the confiscation of all Church properties, the parish clergy being supported by the state treasury.[168] One by one, the states forming the Papal territory were then overrun by his armies and annexed to United Italy. The capture of Rome itself in 1870 put a definite end to the Papal territorial possessions whose revenues had been the chief support of the central government of the Church. The Holy Father was now forced to appeal to the generosity of the faithful throughout the world, and, to their credit, these have always been most liberal in their response.[169]

In the states under the Austrian rule, the Church suffered the loss of fully one-third of her monasteries through the misguided attempts at Church reform, undertaken by Emperor Joseph II in 1781.[170] But a considerable portion of the proceeds of this confiscation was used to endow new parishes where these were needed.[171] Outside of this, the

---

[164] Sampson, *op. cit.*, p. 233.
[165] Sampson, *op. cit.*, pp. 227 and 229.
[166] Funk, *Lehrbuch der Kirchengeschichte*, II, 885.
[167] Funk, *op. cit.*, II, 927.
[168] *Ibidem.*
[169] Funk, *op. cit.*, II, 954.
[170] Funk, *op. cit.*, II, 825.
[171] *Ibidem.*

financial status of the Austrian Church remained about the same as before.

In Spain and Portugal the Church received back practically all of her property, after the expulsion of the French in 1813. Several revolutions, accompanied by the inevitable suppression of monasteries and the confiscation of ecclesiastical properties, followed each other in rapid succession in these countries, and it was not until 1875 that tranquility was restored. Since then the Spanish Church has been able to exercise her rights in comparative peace. In Portugal, however, the revolution of 1911, which resulted in the formation of a republican form of government, was accompanied by the separation of Church and State, the spoliation of the Church, and the passing of laws retricting her independence and her rights in regard to property. These laws were, however, considerably ameliorated in 1918, when a compromise was effected with the Holy See.[172]

After the partition of Poland in the eighteenth century, in those sections which were annexed by Russia, the Church had to undergo an almost uninterrupted persecution until the time of the World War. Her religious houses were suppressed, her property confiscated, the religious and the secular clergy, for the greater part, banished, and her children often forced to join the Orthodox Church.[173] One of the few beneficial results of the late war has been the re-establishment of the independence of Poland and the restoration of her rights and independence to the Catholic Church in Poland.

The opening of the nineteenth century was a time of disaster for the Church in southern Germany, in regard to her temporal possessions. In the Treaty of Luneville in 1801, which ended the war with France, "it was decided that the principalities and possessions of the Church should be in part made over to France and in part secularized, to indemnify the civil princes for their territorial losses on the left bank of the Rhine." [174] The German Princes were

[172] Funk, *op. cit.*, II, 930.
[173] Funk, *op. cit.*, II, 938-939.
[174] Alzog, *Man. of Univ. Ch. Hist.*, III, 676.

empowered in 1803 to take over all the property of the Church in their lands, including the monastic foundations, for their own use.[175] Thus, at one stroke, the wealthiest Church in Christendom was impoverished and her numerous scholastic and charitable institutions almost totally destroyed.[176]

In the Concordat with Napoleon it was stipulated that these states, which had profited by this confiscation, were to support the clergy from the State funds. This agreement has also been observed by the Prussian State which succeeded Napoleon in the government of these lands.[177] Laws were, however, passed at various times, limiting the income of the Church and the size of the donations which she might accept, thus preventing the reestablishment of any considerable endowments.[178] With the formation of the German Republic in 1918, separation of Church and State was introduced, with a consequent loss of the State support.[179] The Church received some recompense for this loss by being given full liberty to acquire and hold any property that may be donated to her in any way whatever. During the last years Concordats between the Holy See and some of the German States have led to a partial restoration of this State support.

In the other countries of Europe, during modern times, the Church has had to depend almost entirely on the voluntary gifts of her children for her support, as the governments offer her no aid and the Catholics have generally been too poor and few in number to establish any considerable endowments. Sometimes they were even compelled to help maintain the non-Catholic State religion, not only through the payment of taxes, but even by the payment of tithes directly to these churches. Thus, in Ireland, the Catholics paid tithes, amounting to about fifteen million dollars annually, towards the support of the Anglican Church establishment in Ireland. Two thousand Anglican

---

175 *Ibidem.*

176 Funk, *Lehrbuch der Kirchengeschichte*, II, 899.

177 Vogt, *Kirchliches Vermögensrecht*, pp. 119-120.

178 Vogt, *op. cit.*, p. 17 et seq.

179 Funk, *op. cit.*, II, 974.

ministers, some of whom had not a single soul under their charge, divided among themselves this revenue.[180] In the County of Kilkenny there were 380,000 Catholics and about 1,000 Anglicans. Yet the former "were forced to pay an Anglican bishop and sixty-four ministers a sum which made their income, in legal tithes, equal to six times that received by the Catholic clergy through voluntary contributions." [181]

Conditions being such, it is not surprising to learn that movements were repeatedly set on foot for the abolition of the tithes.[182] This the British Government refused to permit, offering instead a subsidy to the Catholic Church. The Irish episcopacy declined this support, bitter experience having shown that it was preferable to be poor but free rather than well provided for but subject to interference from a non-Catholic government.[183] Finally, in 1838, the tithes were abolished; in 1845, the Church's right to hold property was acknowledged; and in 1869, a part of the stolen possessions was restored to the Catholic Church.[184]

In the American countries, south of the United States, the Church was comparatively rich as long as she remained under the protection of the mother-countries, Spain and Portugal. The lands were dotted with numerous well-endowed monasteries and charitable institutions.[185] But when these countries asserted their independence, an age of sporadic revolutions set in, which have continued, more or less, in the various countries up to the present time. During this period of independence of these states, the fortunes of the Church have varied. The overthrow of the existing government was generally accompanied by the persecution and spoliation of the Church.[186] As a result she has lost most of her property and is dependent for her support

---

180 Alzog, *Man. of Univ. Ch. Hist.*, III, 729.

181 *Ibidem.*

182 Alzog, *Man. of Univ. Ch. Hist.*, III, 729.

183 Alzog, *op. cit.*, III, 737.

184 Funk, *Lehrbuch der Kirchengeschichte*, II, 934.

185 Baring, "Ledgers of the Royal Treasurers of Spanish-America in the Sixteenth Century," *The Hispanic American Historical Review*, II (1919), 182-187.

186 Funk, *op. cit.*, II, 946.

either on the State, or where the State is hostile, on the uncertain contributions of the faithful.

The beginning of modern times also marks the development of a new method of Church support, namely, pew-rent. Seats for the comfort of the worshippers were first introduced into the body of the church building during the thirteenth century.[187] At first, individuals would build these seats for themselves, in any part of the church they pleased. This haphazard erection of seats by individual parishioners led to much confusion and trouble, the aisles often being left too narrow or even blocked altogether, and the seats of those in front sometimes preventing those who were behind them from seeing the altar because of the height of these seats.[188] After a period of evolution and legislation, continuing into the sixteenth century, these seats were customarily erected by the parish, and definite places appointed, rented or sold to the individual parishioners.[189] In spite of some abuses, to which this custom of renting pews has led, it has maintained itself in many places, and sometimes is the source of a considerable, or even of the major, part of the parish income.[190] The Church has never definitely approved of the custom; on the contrary, she has tried to have it abolished, if feasible.[191]

One of the most consoling factors in modern Catholic life is the widespread interest which the faithful in general are beginning to take in the missions. During the course of the last century, innumerable societies have sprung up whose members seek to help the missionaries by their prayers and financial support.[192] Such manifestations of the spirit of true charity deserve all possible encouragement, for they furnish the best proof of the continued vitality of the Church and of the active faith of her children. Nor need there be any apprehension that these Catholics, who show themselves generous in their support of the missions, will

---

[187] Vogt, *Kirchliches Vermögensrecht*, p. 80.

[188] Grünewald, *Die Rechtsverhältnisse an Kirchenstühlen*, p. 4.

[189] Grünewald, *op. cit.*, p. 5.

[190] Grünewald, *op. cit.*, p. 10.

[191] Grünewald, *op. cit.*, p. 12 and note 3 on p. 13.

[192] Funk, *Lehrbuch der Kirchengeschichte*, II, 977.

lessen their contributions to their own parish. Experience has shown that such Catholics are the best supporters of their parishes.

5.—Church Support in the United States

The credit for laying the foundations of the Catholic Church in the Thirteen Colonies belongs to the Jesuit Fathers. In 1632, when about to found his colony in Maryland, Lord Baltimore applied to the provincial of the Jesuits in England for several priests to accompany his colonists.[193] He warned them, however, that they would have to provide for their own support, as he himself was unable to promise them any salary, and his settlers would be too poor to hold out any hope of their being able to contribute anything.

Lord Baltimore had announced that every settler, who would pay for the transportation to the new colony of a certain number of artisans or farmers, would receive a specified acreage of land as a grant. So "it was decided (by the Jesuit community in England) that two fathers were to go as gentlemen adventurers...acquiring land like others, from which they were to draw their support." [194] These lands, and others subsequently obtained in the same way, were to form the main source of revenue for the clergy in Maryland for almost two hundred years.

The first colonists appreciated the self-sacrificing spirit of these Jesuit fathers and, as soon as their means permitted, were as liberal in their contributions as possible. Numerous legacies and bequests were made to the Church, represented by these Jesuit missionaries, before the eighteenth century. A converted Indian chief, Maquacomen, made the first donation of which a record is available. In 1640 he bestowed on the mission a substantial tract of land, "so fertile that its produce was the main reliance of the Maryland missionaries." [195]

---

193 Shea, *The Catholic Church in the U. S.*, I, 38.
194 *Ibidem.*
195 Shea, *op. cit.*, II, 49.

Owing, however, to various causes, the Catholics began to grow indifferent, and to ignore their duty of supporting the Church. In an account of the condition of religion in Maryland, in 1790, Bishop Carroll had to state that "Catholics contributed nothing to the support of religion or its ministers; the whole charge of their maintenance, of furnishing the altars, of all traveling expenses, fell on the priests themselves, and no compensation was ever offered for any service performed by them..." [196]

This condition of affairs was due to various causes. The colonial government had fallen into the hands of those who were hostile to the Church, and who resorted to oppressive measures against the Catholics. Disproportionately heavy taxes and large pecuniary fines were imposed upon them. As a result, many were unable to contribute any substantial sums to the Church, while others became discouraged and began to neglect their religious duties. Then also, owing to the scarcity of priests and the great distances separating the various plantations and settlements, few Catholics were able to fulfill their religious duties, were able to attend the Sunday Mass and receive the Sacraments with any degree of regularity. This, combined with the results of the persecution, led to a gradual indifference towards religion which threatened to utterly destroy the infant Church in Maryland.[197]

Bishop Carroll realized that if the Church was to continue and grow the Catholics would have to provide for its support. He realized also that the mere fact that they had built and were maintaining a church in their own neighborhood would offer a strong incentive to the members of the parish to remain faithful to their religion. In the first synod, which he held in Baltimore in 1791, he, therefore, urged all Catholics to fulfill their duty and help maintain the Church by their voluntary contributions.[198]

---

[196] Shea, *op. cit.*, II, 49, quoting from "Relatio pro Eminentissimo Cardinali Antonelli de statu religionis in Unitis Foed. Americae provinciis," Feb. 27, 1785.

[197] Shea, *op. cit.*, II, 47-49.

[198] Acta et Statuta Synodi Dioec. Balt. (1791), c. 23—*Coll. Lac.*, III, 6.

As Catholics settled in neighboring colonies, the Jesuit fathers of Maryland extended their ministrations to these settlements. In 1740, Pennsylvania appears in the records of the Society of Jesus as a distinct mission.[199] Here also the missionaries at first supported themselves, as they had done in Maryland. But it was not long before the Catholics, although most of them were yet comparatively poor, "contributed money to erect and maintain churches and support the priest who attended them." [200] The same process took place in most of the colonial settlements where the Church was established. Missionaries who came to minister to the Catholics at first supported themselves, or were maintained by outside help. Very quickly, however, these communities would become self-supporting, and would then furnish a focus, often also a portion of the material means, for the extension of missionary activities to other localities.

In the southern portions of what are now the United States, lands formerly belonging to Spain, priests accompanied all expeditions to new territories, and immediately set about establishing missions.[201] "Generous provision was made by the rulers of Spain for the support of the clergy (in these territories) and the maintenance of religion." [202] The system of tithes, which was in force in Spain, was also introduced in these territories, and continued in use as long as the territories remained Spanish possessions.[203]

The tithing system was also introduced in the French territories in the north and in the Mississippi Valley. Even after France lost these lands to England, in 1762, this custom was upheld, for by the "Quebec Act" of 1774, "the parish priest had a legal title to his tithes in Michigan, Indiana, Illinois, Wisconsin, and by parity, at Natchez and Mobile." [204] When these lands, as also those of Spain in the south, were acquired by the independent United States, the policy of separation of Church and State brought about

---

199 Shea, *The Catholic Church in the U. S.*, I, 389.

200 Shea, *op. cit.*, I, 452.

201 MacCaffrey, *History of the Church from the Renaissance to the Reformation*, I, 268.

202 *Ibidem.*

203 Shea, *op. cit.*, I, pp. 158 and 499.

204 Shea, *op. cit.*, II, 135.

the abolition of these legal tithes. Voluntary donations, under one form or another, were to form the chief support of the Church, until such a time when she will be able to establish endowments.

The American Church will always owe a debt of gratitude to the Catholic Church in foreign lands for the generous help which was extended to her during these early years. Almost without exception, the original establishment of the Church, in the various sections of the country, was made possible through the financial aid obtained from foreign lands. As has already been indicated, the Spanish rulers, from their own means, donated generously to establish the Church in Florida, Texas, New Mexico, Arizona and California.[205] The missions, in the lands subject to France, were also established by means contributed by the state treasury of France, or by donations from private persons in France.[206]

In the English colonies, the establishment of the Church is due to the initial aid offered by the Jesuit community in England. These had furnished the necessary means for the transportation of the missionaries and of the artisans and farmers whom they brought along in order to enable them to apply for grants of land.[207] The parishes in Pennsylvania, for a long time, received greatly needed help from a fund which an English Catholic had founded, in 1670, for their benefit.[208] As the Church spread to new territories, hardly a single diocese was founded whose first churches were not partly or entirely paid for by money obtained in other countries. Missionaries, in writing to their friends or relatives in Europe, would stress the crying need for funds to erect churches in the communities they served, and generally they succeeded in obtaining aid. Parishes and dioceses applied for financial help to the "Association for the Propagation of the Faith," to the "Leopoldine Association," or to some other European missionary society,

---

[205] Cf. Shea, *op. cit.*, I, pp. 157, 195 and 499.

[206] Shea, *op. cit.*, I, 219 and 547.

[207] Shea, *op. cit.*, II, 48.

[208] Shea, *op. cit.*, I, 384-385.

generally not in vain. Religious institutions were erected and equipped by the European houses from which they originated.

For its continued existence, the Church is, as yet, almost entirely dependent on the continued voluntary contributions of its members. The Catholic Church in the United States is still in the formative period. The establishment of new parishes, the dividing or combining of existing parishes, are daily occurrences. Then, also, the Catholics of this country are, in large numbers, immigrants or the first descendants of immigrants from all the different countries of Europe. Many of these, coming from lands where the Church is well-endowed, or where she is supported by state taxation, do not realize how dependent the Church, in this country, is on their contributions for its existence. The pastors are, therefore, often compelled to resort to all possible methods of raising funds. That they have sometimes resorted to measures which cannot be held up as worthy of imitation can easily be condoned, to some extent at least, when their desperate financial needs are understood.

Up to the present time, no uniform system of Church support has been generally adopted. The collection, taken up during the parochial Masses on Sundays, as prescribed by the First Synod of Baltimore,[209] is everywhere employed. A different form of this collection, the weekly or the monthly envelope collection, is rapidly increasing in popularity during the last years.[210] The people are asked to place their contribution, a certain fixed sum, or a certain percentage of their income, in envelopes which are stamped with their names or with identifying numbers, so that a record of the contributions of the individual members of the parish may be kept. In some places, the seat-collection has also been introduced, generally replacing the pew-rent system. Various combinations or duplications of these collections have been introduced in some churches. Instances are even known where ushers pass around three times dur-

---

[209] Acta et Statuta Synodi Dioec. Balt. (1791), c. 23—*Coll. Lac.*, III, 6.

[210] Jansen, "Church Support," *Hom. and Past. Rev.*, XXVIII (1927), 267.

ing every Mass, the seat-collection, the envelope collection, and the loose-change plate collection being taken up in succession. Whether such methods are advisable or productive of a greater income, over an extended period of time, cannot be definitely determined.

Special collections are also taken up on certain days at the instance of the Holy See or of the local ordinary for certain definite purposes, such as the maintenance of the Church in the Holy Land, the support of the Holy See (Peter's Pence), the maintenance of national or diocesan institutions, etc. Mention may also be made here of the door-collection, ushers at the entry of the church, asking all those who enter to contribute a certain set sum.

Besides these collections many other methods have been used, or are still in use, to increase the revenues of the Church. In some places, a tentative budget is drawn up, and an assessment made upon the parishioners according to their wealth. Special assessments are also resorted to for the purpose of meeting extraordinary expenses. House to house collections are made by the pastor, or by someone appointed by the pastor, going from one family to another in the parish, and begging or cajoling them to give substantial sums. The paying of pew rent is a very common practice, although it seems to be slowly dying out.[211]

Societies, such as the Christian Mothers, the Sodality of the Blessed Virgin, the Young Men's Society, etc., often have been regarded as added sources of income. Card parties, dinners, teas, bazaars, fairs, picnics, and even dances, under the auspices of the parish or of some society, are frequently resorted to; lotteries, great and small, are held to raise funds. An historical instance of the use of a lottery is found in the building of the Baltimore Cathedral in 1803. 21,000 tickets, at ten dollars each, were sold; eighty-five per cent of the proceeds were distributed in prizes, and the remaining part applied to the building fund.[212] Chain letters have been sent out by pastors, or by the heads of institutions, the recipients of these letters being

---

[211] Jansen, *op. cit.*, p. 266.

[212] Shea, *The Catholic Church in the U. S.*, II, 600-601.

asked to send in a small sum, and also send a certain number of copies of the appeal to his friends. Begging letters, sent to every Catholic whose name can be obtained by fair means or foul, are even now very commonly used. Fortunately such means are not so imperative any more as they were formerly. "To be a pastor in those days required an unlimited amount of effrontery to be able to stand before the same congregation every Sunday, threatening and cajoling, in order to wheedle another dollar out of the pocket of the parishioners to meet some pressing financial need." [213]

An adaptation of the tithing system is being tried out in a number of places. In 1927, the Catholics of the Diocese of Seattle were asked to give four per cent of their income in an envelope, no loose money being accepted.[214] Des Moines Diocese adopted the voluntary payment of the full tithes, a few years earlier.[215] In Elkhart, Indiana, this same system of tithes was introduced in 1915, with apparently very good results.[216] The success of these tentative trials would seem to indicate that the people are as generous as they ever were, provided they understand the needs of the Church and feel that they are not being imposed upon. It may be hoped that these attempts are the forerunners of a uniform method for the insurance of a stable and ample income for the Church, thereby precluding the necessity of the execrated money-talks which only too frequently have replaced the Sunday sermon.

---

[213] Jansen, "Church Support," *Hom. and Past. Rev.*, XXVIII (1927), 267.

[214] *Ibidem.*

[215] *Ibidem.*

[216] Jansen, *op. cit.*, p. 269.

CHAPTER TWO

The Obligation of Church Support

1.—Source of Obligation

The obligation of the faithful to support the Church has its basis in the natural law. Every person who devotes his time and energy to the giving of an actual and necessary service to others has a natural right to expect a suitable recompense, which will enable him to support himself and prosecute his work. To even suggest that a physician or a teacher should render his services gratis, and support himself by his own productive labor, would be regarded as a sign of lunacy. Complaints, indeed, are sometimes heard that one or another class of public servants demand a compensation entirely out of proportion to the service which it renders, or that it is not giving any service for which it might expect to be supported. But these very complaints testify to the common belief in the equity of the rule, that "the laborer is worthy of his hire." [1]

The mission of the Church is to pray for, to instruct, to minister to, and to offer up the Divine Service for mankind.[2] That she thereby renders a real service is acknowledged by everyone who becomes a member of the Church. By joining the Church he shows that he considers her help necessary if he is to attain his ultimate end, the glorification of God through the saving of his own soul. Since the Church needs temporal means to carry on her mission, she has an undeniable right, based on the natural law, to demand that those who benefit by her services furnish her with the necessary means.

---

[1] *Lk.*, X, 7.

[2] Conc. Plen. Balt. III, n. 264.

The binding force of this natural law is further strengthened by the Divine positive law. At the same time that God, on Mount Sinai, established the Jewish Dispensation, He also decreed that those whom He had chosen to serve Him in the Temple and to minister to the people were to be supported by the contributions of the people. The Levite Aaron and his descendants were to be priests,[3] while the other Levites were to be their assistants and servants in the discharge of the religious functions and ceremonies.[4] In the division of the conquered lands the tribe of Levi, at the express command of God,[5] did not receive a portion,[6] but the other tribes, in proportion to their wealth, were to cede to them forty-eight cities in various parts of the country to dwell in,[7] and support them by making certain specified offerings, chief of which were the tithes and first-fruits.[8]

In the New Testament Christ reaffirmed this commandment. When He sent forth His disciples to go and preach His Gospel to the people, He instructed them not to take along any money or supplies, but to depend on the people to whom they were preaching for sustenance and clothing.[9] He Himself also placed the mark of His approval upon the law, prescribing the support of religion, by paying the customary dues to the Temple,[10] although He maintained that He and His Apostles were free from this law, since it was their mission to preach, and, therefore, they themselves had a right to receive this support. The very fact, however, that He insisted on their freedom from this law, indicates that He recognized and approved it as binding upon all who were not called to devote themselves to the special works of religion.

---

[3] *Ex.*, XXVIII, 1 and XL, 12; *Num.*, XVIII, 1 and 7.

[4] *Num.*, VIII, 6-26, and XVIII, 2-6.

[5] *Num.*, XVIII, 20.

[6] *Jos.*, XIII, 14 and 33.

[7] *Num.*, XXXV, 1-8.

[8] *Lev.*, XXVII, 30; *Num.*, XV, 10-21; *Num.*, XVIII, 21; *Deut.*, XVIII, 1-8.

[9] *Mt.*, X, 9-10; *Lk.*, X, 4-7.

[10] *Mt.*, XVII, 23-26.

When St. Paul wishes to prove his zeal for the Gospel, he reminds his Corinthian converts that he has never asked them to support him,[11] although, as he points out, he would have been fully justified, both by the natural [12] and divine law, in insisting that they do so, for "the Lord ordained that they who preach the Gospel, should live by the Gospel." [13] In the same letter he orders weekly collections to be taken up in the churches of Corinth, just as he had ordered in Galatia, for the use of the Church in other localities.[14] The reason for the paucity of references in the New Testament to this obligation is easily found. The Jewish people had always been accustomed to the payment of the tithes as an obligation. When they became Christians, the only change in the obligation was that the tithes were paid to the Christian community instead of to the Temple. The members of the first community at Jerusalem even went to the length of placing all their property at the disposal of the Church.[15] Converts from paganism, having shown themselves willing to sacrifice their standing in the world, even their very lives, if necessary, would hardly be less willing to contribute to the maintenance and spread of their new found faith. That the early Christians were, in fact, very generous, can hardly be doubted.[16] Consequently there was no occasion for stressing the obligation.

But whenever she has found it necessary the Church has not hesitated to remind the faithful of this obligation, and to enforce it through her own legislation. From the second century onwards various bishops [17] have called the atten-

---

[11] I *Cor.*, IX, 12 and 13.

[12] I *Cor.*, IX, 7.

[13] I *Cor.*, IX, 14.

[14] I *Cor.*, XVI, 1-2.

[15] Acts, IV, 34-35.

[16] Gasquet, *Parish Life in Medieval England*, p. 10; Clarke, *History of Tithes*, p. 4.

[17] St. Cyprian (+258), *De Oper. et Eleemos.—MPL*, IV, 609; also St. Irenaeus (+190), St. Ambrose and St. Augustine, according to Alzog, *Man. of Univ. Ch. Hist.*, I, 658.

tion of their charges to this duty, sharply rebuking those who were remiss.[18] The Apostolical Constitutions [19] prescribe very definitely how and what amounts the Christians were to contribute. Although this work is the production of a private person, it, nevertheless, serves to indicate what the common belief was as to the binding force of this obligation at the time of its composition.[20] It is very explicit as to the foundation upon which this obligation of support is based. "So, therefore, shalt thou do as the Lord has appointed, and shalt give to the priest what things are due to him,. . . as to the mediator between God and such as stand in need of purgation and forgiveness. For it is thy duty to give, and his to administer. . . ." [21]

The obligation of Church support has also been the subject matter of a considerable proportion of the synodal legislation of the Church. The Council of Macon, which was held in 585, was among the first to make express mention of it. The fathers of this Council, declaring that it was their duty, and the purpose of the Council, to reform Catholic life and custom, which in the course of time (and because of the confusion brought about in society and government by the migration of nations), had sadly deteriorated, laid particular stress upon the necessity of making the faithful realize their duty to contribute their proportionate share to the support of the Church. Then only, as they point out, will the clergy be able to devote their time to prayer and the spiritual ministry, and to effectual work in the relief of the wants of the poor, and the redemption of captives.[22] As a proportionate share, which the faithful were to contribute, the Council commanded the payment of tithes, declaring that this proportion has been determined by God, and had, in past centuries, been customarily ob-

---

18 E.g., St. Cyprian, *loc. cit.*

19 *Apost. Constit.*, II, 35; VII, 29, and VIII, 30—*MPG*, I, 541 et seq.

20 Probable date of composition of the *Apostolical Constitutions* is around the year 400. Cf. Bardenhewer, *Patrology*, p. 350.

21 *Apost. Constit.*, II, 35—*MPG*, I, 541.

22 C. Matisc., c. 5—*Mansi*, IX, 952.

served throughout the Church.[23] During the following centuries numerous councils enacted similar decrees.[24]

The obligation of supporting the Church is also stressed in the Decretals of Gregory IX, an authentic [25] collection of laws for the universal Church, up to 1918. These Decretals bound the faithful to a strict observance of the payment of tithes:

> Volumus ergo et districte praecipimus, quatenus, antequam ullas deducatis de cunctis vestris bonis praedictis expensas, salvis privilegiis Romanae ecclesiae decimas ecclesiis, ad quas pertinent, cum integritate debita persolvatis.[26]

Rules are laid down specifying very accurately who must pay the tithes, to whom, when, and what tithes and first-fruits are to be paid, and what temporal and spiritual penalties, including even excommunication, may be employed to enforce these payments.[27] Further decrees, enforcing this same obligation of Church support, are to be found in later collections, and in the legislation of councils.[28] These laws remained in force up to the promulgation of the Code, although in many countries, due to changes of time and

---

[23] *Ibidem.*

[24] C. Turonensis, Littera Synodalis (567)—*Mansi,* IX, 808; C. Rothomagense (649), can. 3—*Mansi,* X, 1200; C. Trullonis (692), can. 28—*Mansi,* XI, 955; C. Calchutense (787), can. 17—*Mansi,* XII, 947; C. Aurelatense VI (813), can. 9—*Mansi,* XIV, 60; C. Moguntiacum (813), can. 38—*Mansi,* XIV, 73; C. Rhemense II (813), can. 38—*Mansi,* XIV, 81; C. Turonense III (813), can. 9—*Mansi,* XIV, 85; C. Suessionense II (853), can. 9—*Mansi,* XIV, 981; C. Valentinum III (855), can. 10—*Mansi,* XV, 9; C. Wormatiense (868), can. 59—*Mansi,* XV, 879; C. Troslejanum (909), cap. IV-VI—*Mansi,* XVIIIa, 273; C. Bundense (943), cap. II—*Mansi,* XVIIIa, 399; C. Tolosanum (1119), can. 4—*Mansi,* XXI, 227; C. Rhemense (1148), can. 8—*Mansi,* XXI, 716; C. Cassiliense (1172), can. 3—*Mansi,* XXII, 134; C. Londoniense (1200), can. 9—*Mansi,* XXII, 718; C. Burdegalense (1255), cap. XIII—*Mansi,* XXIII, 861; C. Eboracense (1367), can. 5—*Mansi,* XXVI, 465.

[25] Maroto, *Institutiones Iuris Canonici,* I, 75.

[26] C. 22, X, *De Decimis, Primitiis et Oblationibus,* III, 30.

[27] C. 1-35, X, *De Decimis, Primitiis et Oblationibus,* III, 30.

[28] E.g., *De Decimis, Primitiis et Oblationibus,* III, 13, in VI°; Conc. Trid., sess. XXI, *De ref.,* c. 4; sess. XXIV, *De ref.,* c. 13, and sess. XXV, *De ref.,* c. 12.

circumstances, custom had abrogated the various prescriptions of these laws.[29]

A comparison between the present and the former legislation will show that great changes have been made in the laws relating to Church support. In the former the Church laid down very specific rules in regard to this obligation, and enforced them by penalties, if necessary. The present Code does not contain a single sanction directly enforcing this obligation. It merely states that local statutes and customs are to be observed.

Canon 1502.—Ad decimarum et primitiarum solutionem quod attinet, peculiaria statuta ac laudabiles consuetudines in unaquaque regione serventur.

The reason for this change of policy may be found in the altered circumstances which would render the prescription of a uniform system of support for the entire Church not only useless but unenforceable. During the Middle Ages, society throughout Europe, to which Continent the Church was practically limited, was far more homogeneous than that of the various countries to which she now has spread. One form of civil government, the feudal system, held sway wherever the Church was established; and throughout these lands the relations between the Church and the states were practically the same.[30] As a consequence, a single, uniform system of support could be prescribed for the entire Church.

Today the Church is established in various countries, under greatly dissimilar conditions; in countries under a Catholic or a hostile government, and in others where the government tries, as much as possible, to ignore her very existence. In some nations she is maintained, to a greater or lesser extent, by State aid or by endowments, while in others she has to depend upon the contributions of the faithful for all that she needs. To outline and prescribe the use

[29] Vermeersch-Creusen, *Epitome I. C.* II, no. 824; Wernz, *Ius Decretalium,* III, Tit. VIII, no. 1-2.

[30] For a description of the state of European society, in the Middle Ages, cf. Davis, *Life on a Medieval Barony, a Picture of a Typical Feudal Community in the 13th Century;* also Belloc, *Europe and the Faith,* and *How the Reformation Happened;* also Kurth-Day, *The Church at the Turning Points of History,* p. 94 et seq.

of a single and uniform system of support for the Church in all these countries is manifestly impossible.

Another reason for the change in policy may be adduced. The purpose underlying all ecclesiastical laws is the attainment of discipline and good order in the Church, as a means to further her ultimate purpose, the saving of souls. Since voluntary good works are ordinarily far more meritorious and, therefore, of greater service to the individual in the attainment of salvation than such as are performed under duress, the Church must necessarily prefer that the contributions of the faithful be voluntary rather than enforced, as taxes or assessments. And if these voluntary donations are sufficient to enable the Church to fulfill her mission, she will be only too willing to refrain from compulsory legislation. At the present time, this seems to be the happy condition of affairs in many countries.[31]

This was not always true during past centuries. Various causes, such as the downfall of the Roman Empire of the West, and the consequent demoralization of the entire social structure; the threatening of a return to barbarism, and the great disorders preceding and attending the reestablishment of society on a feudal basis; the too close union, if it may be called such, and even the practical amalgamation of the ecclesiastical with the civil government,[32] which, at various times, furthered the introduction of certain abuses into the system of temporalities of the Church,[33] or which led the people to include the Church in their resentment of the injustice of civil rulers; these and other causes, at various times and in various combinations, tended to lessen the generosity of the faithful.

During these ages the Church also had to demand a greater proportion of the total income of the people than she now does. She had to provide for many needs, which in our times are, to a great extent, financed by the State or by private individuals. Hospitals and homes for the

---

[31] Doheny, *Church Property, Modes of Acquisition*, p. 30.

[32] Cf. Pöschl, *Bischofsgut und Mensa Episcopalis*, I, 168 et seq., for a description of this condition and its effects.

[33] *Ibidem;* also Kurth-Day, *The Church at the Turning Points of History*, 58 et seq. and 164.

care of the sick and the diseased, the poor, the aged and orphans,[34] had to be built and supported from her funds. She frequently had to help finance the desperate wars fought to save Western civilization from the incursions of the heathens or the Mohammedans.[35] She lavished her riches in the redemption of those taken prisoners in these wars, or captured by pirates.[36] She conducted the civil government of great territories, and all the necessary officials, including the military forces, were supported from her income.[37] The entire system of education, from the lower schools up to the large universities, was very largely dependent upon her for its maintenance.[38] These and other activities, now provided for in large part by other agencies, required that she have at her disposal a proportionately larger income than she now needs. To obtain this she had to enforce her right of claiming support and specify what part of the people's income she needed.

Because of these reasons the Church has not included any universal law, enforcing Church support, in her present legislation. She does, however, vindicate to herself the right, independent of civil authority, of demanding this support from the faithful, if she should find it necessary.

Canon 1496.—Ecclesiae ius quoque est, independens a civili potestate, exigendi a fidelibus quae ad cultum divinum, ad honestam clericorum aliorumque ministrorum sustentationem et ad reliquos fines sibi proprios sint necessaria.

---

[34] Pöschl, *Bischofsgut und Mensa Episcopalis,* I, 105-113; also Barrett, "The Pre-Reformation Church in Scotland" in the *Am. Cath. Quart. Rev.,* XXIII (1898), 797; Foakes-Jackson, *History of the Christian Church,* p. 581; Funk, *Lehrbuch der Kirchengeschichte,* I, 296. The *Raccolta di Concordati,* p. 530, contains a copy of a letter from the Holy See to the ruler of Parma, 1795, in which the latter is given permission to mortgage or sell Church property, and devote the proceeds to relief work among the poor.

[35] Link, *Mess-Stipendien,* p. 83; Kurth-Day, *op. cit.,* pp. 49 and 104; Freyer, "Der Staat und die Kirchensteuer in Deutschland," *AkKR,* LXXXVII (1907), 407.

[36] Ratzinger, *Geschichte der christlichen Armenpflege,* p. 130.

[37] Pöschl, *Bischofsgut und Mensa Episcopalis,* I, 3-4 and 145 et seq.; Link, *Mess-Stipendien,* p. 83.

[38] Link, *op. cit.,* p. 84; Walsh, *The Thirteenth, Greatest of Centuries,* pp. 71, 73, 22, 26 and 30, etc.

From the very beginning of her existence in the territory of the United States, the Church had to accommodate herself to novel circumstances and difficulties. To have attempted an enforcement of the existing laws on Church support, or any similar laws, would have been almost suicidal. Among the pioneers who rapidly spread westwards through the country were great numbers of Catholics,[39] of whom many, in spite of the heroic labors of the but too few missionary priests, were left, for longer or shorter periods of time, without the ministrations of the Church. The unfortunate consequence was that a large proportion of these lost their faith,[40] and another large portion became indifferent and careless, although they still claimed to be Catholics. Owing to the circumstances of their life, which compelled them to rely almost entirely upon themselves for their material needs and their personal safety, the pioneers became fiercely independent, impatient of even the most necessary and lawful restraint.[41] Any attempt to force these Catholic pioneers, by means of ecclesiastical penalties, to contribute to the establishment and maintenance of the Church in their locality would only have succeeded in causing most of them to sever all connections with the Church, and thus would have defeated the very intention for establishing the Church, viz., the saving of these souls.

With true apostolic spirit,[42] therefore, these missionaries were generally very prudent in enforcing their right to be

---

[39] The following will illustrate the rapidity with which the Church had to grow to accommodate the Catholic pioneers. In 1849, there were about two thousand white people in the territories of Minnesota and the two Dakotas. In 1857, the statistics of the diocese of St. Paul, which included this territory, were: 29 churches, 35 stations, 20 priests and a Catholic population of about 50,000. In 1901, this same territory was divided into one archdiocese and five suffragan dioceses, with 600 priests, and a Catholic population of about 400,000. These data are taken from a sermon delivered by Archbishop Ireland, on July 1, 1901, as contained in *The Diocese of St. Paul, the Golden Jubilee.*

[40] It can hardly be denied that these frontier conditions were responsible, in large measure, for the appalling leakage in the Church, which earnest Catholics have deplored.

[41] Cf. Beard, *The Rise of American Civilization*, I, 527 and 535, for a description of the character of these pioneers.

[42] I *Cor.*, IX, 12-15.

supported by the faithful. They were grateful for the hospitality which was generously and gratuitously extended to them by all,[43] as well as for small donations which they occasionally received. But for the funds necessary to erect and equip churches and to obtain other needed supplies for the church and for themselves, they had to depend largely upon the generosity of their friends at home,[44] and of the various missionary societies established in Europe.[45]

Such sources of support could, however, only be temporary and in the nature of a stop-gap. As the conditions of life in a locality gradually became more normal and the Catholics more numerous and more imbued with the spirit of the Church, they were expected to contribute at least enough to maintain the church in their own locality. But they were often reluctant to accept even this responsibility, and had to be reminded of it again and again. The first ecclesiastical convocation in the United States, the diocesan synod of Baltimore in 1791, found itself forced to stress this obligation and complained especially of the indifference of the more prosperous Catholics regarding the observance of this grave duty.

> Crescente numero Catholicorum,. . .opus est in Vinea Domini multo majore quam olim fuerat operariorum copia, qui tamen obtineri non possunt aut conservari, nisi subsidium pro eorum alimonia a fidelibus conferatur, uti divino praecepto conferre tenentur, dicente Apostolo aequum esse ut qui spiritualia aliis seminant, de carnalibus ipsorum metant. Itaque fideles de hac obligatione frequenter moneantur, cui nisi satisfaciant,

---

[43] Beard, *The Rise of American Civilization,* I, 528.

[44] E.g., Maes, *Life of Father Nerinckx,* pp. 87 and 120.

[45] Cf. the letter of thanks of the First Provincial Council of Baltimore, 1829, to the French Society of the Propagation of the Faith; Nona Congregatio Privata—*Coll. Lac.,* III, 16; also the letter of the Fathers of the Seventh Provincial Council of Baltimore, May 13th, 1849, to the Leopoldine Society of Austria, acknowledging the great help which they had extended to the Church in America—*Coll. Lac.,* III, 118.

sibi ipsis debent imputare quod neque Dominicis et festis diebus Missam audiant, neque Sacramentorum in summis suis necessitatibus fiant participes. Unde quando pro mensura temporalium bonorum sibi a Deo concessorum, ad salutis ministerium conferre renuunt, adeoque praecepta divina et ecclesiastica non implent sua culpa, sciant se versari in statu peccati, indignos esse reconciliationis in poenitentiae tribunali obtinendae, neque tantum de suis peccatis rationem Deo reddituros, sed etiam de illorum pauperum crassa ignorantia, ac vitiis, qui propter ditiorum miseram parcimoniam instructionis Christianae manent omnino expertes.[46]

In his pastoral letter of May 28th, 1792, Bishop Carroll again called the attention of all Catholics to this obligation.[47] He said that up to then, in most cases, the clergy in Maryland and Pennsylvania had supported themselves from the products of farms which they had acquired. Owing to the rapid spread of the Church, due to immigration, this course could not be adopted generally and the faithful were in duty bound to contribute to the erection and maintenance of churches and the support of the clergy. Indifference to this duty, he declared, was one of the chief obstructions to the spread of the Church.

Insistence on this obligation is an ever-recurring note in the history of the American Church. In 1813, Bishop Flaget began a visitation of his diocese, Bardstown, Kentucky, and "at every station insisted on a regular and definite support for the priest." [48] When some of the faithful showed a disposition to refuse to contribute to this support, he enforced his command by threatening to cut them off from the Church.[49] Again and again, in provincial councils and in diocesan synods, was this obligation impressed

---

[46] Acta et Statuta Synodi Dioec. Balt., a 1791, n. 23—*Coll. Lac.*, III, 6.

[47] Shea, *The Cath. Ch. in the U. S.*, II, 396; cf. also III, 495.

[49] *Ibidem.*

[48] Shea, *op. cit.*, III, 277.

on the faithful, both before[50] and after the promulgation of the new codification.[51]

2.—Gravity of the Obligation

It is, therefore, undeniable that the faithful are bound to support religion, not only by the natural and the divine law, but also by ecclesiastical law. The common teaching of authors[52] that *per se* this obligation binds gravely, because of the importance of its object, the supplying of the Church with the necessary means for the prosecution of its mission. But if sufficient means are provided by revenues from Church property, or by State aid, or from some other sources, and there is no positive ecclesiastical law or custom enforcing certain special dues, as for instance, the tithes or the first-fruits, the faithful can hardly be compelled to contribute further means which the Church does not need.[53] Such a state of affairs was formerly very prevalent in Europe, and still exists to some extent.

In our country the Church does not occupy such a position. Consequently her members are actually bound to provide for the needs of the Church. The enforcement of this precept in individual cases is, however, very difficult. Kenrick declares that a person who refuses to fulfill his obligation of supporting the Church cannot be judged to be guilty of mortal sin as long as his refusal does not place the clergy in actual need, or inflict too great a burden upon

---

50 Conc. Prov. Cincinn. III (1861), Tertia Congregatio Privata—*Coll. Lac.*, III, 220-221; Conc. Plen. Balt. III, n. 264; Statuta Dioecesis Oklahomensis (1913), n. 18 and 186; Synodus Dioec. Natchetensis V (1886), n. 52; Diocesan Synod of St. Louis (1850), n. 22; Diocesan Synod V of New Orleans (1889), n. 76.

51 Diocesan Synod of Crookston (1921), n. 407; Synodal Decrees of the Diocese of St. Cloud (1924), n. 79; Syn. Dioec. Buff. (1924), Art. 495; Diocesan Statutes of Harrisburg VIII (1928), n. 367; Syn. Dioec. Sti. Ludovici Septima (1929), n. 161.

52 Kenrick, *Theol. Moralis*, IV, n. 64; Suarez, *Opera Omnia*, XIII, cap. 5, n. 6; Noldin, *Summa Theologiae Moralis*, II, 716; Cappello, *De Visitatione*, I, 173.

53 Noldin, *op. cit.*, II, 716; Suarez, *Opera Omnia*, XIII, cap. 5, n. 1; St. Thomas, *Summa*, 2. 2. q. 87, art. 1; S. C. de Prop. Fide, 1 Apr., 1816—*Coll.*, n. 712.

the other faithful.[54] Confessors should, therefore, be very slow to deny sacramental absolution to such a delinquent, even though he remain obstinate. If this refusal should be due to a desire to show contempt for the law, or for the superiors, or if it should cause grave scandal, it might become gravely sinful. The confessor would then be bound to refuse absolution, if the person were not penitent, not because of his refusal to support the Church, but because of the expressed contempt or of the scandal. However, in all matters relating to the obligations of Church support, the confessor must exercise great caution. The Third Plenary Council of Baltimore addressed a very sharp rebuke to clerics who were unduly harsh in urging this precept.

> Fama fert (quae utinam inanis mendaxque sit) nonnullis in locis inveniri sacerdotes qui, ubi gravis culpa non apparet, sacramentalis absolutionis beneficium denegant fidelibus, qui nolint collectis stipem dare, ad quam sub peccato gravi teneri non constet; imo etiam (quod longe detestabilius est) aegrotantibus ac morti proximis adsistere ac sacramenta praebere recusant. Vix animum inducere possumus, ut quidpiam tam atrox et indignum de ecclesiarum nostrarum ministris suspicemur. Si quis vero existat, qui tale quid attentaverit, memores sint Episcopi se muneri suo graviter deesse, nisi in reum pro merito animadvertant.[55]

This strong condemnation may have been inspired, in part, by the peremptory reply of the S. Congregation of the Propaganda to a question proposed from an American diocese:

> Licetne spirituale ministerium denegare iis, aut personis ad illorum spectantibus familiam, v.g., infantibus sacramentum Baptismi, si huic debito se submittere recusent? Resp: Indignam viro ecclesiastico, et animadversione dignam quaestionem de sacris et ipso

---

[54] *Theologia Moralis*, Tract. IV, n. 64; cf. also Noldin, *op. cit.*, II, 716; S. C. de Prop. Fide, 13 Maii, 1816, n. 3—*Coll.*, n. 713.

[55] Con. Plen. Balt. III, n. 292.

> Baptismate denegandis iis qui oblationum debito se submittere recusant.[56]

In the light of these two utterances, for a pastor or a confessor to attempt the enforcement, on his own authority, of the precept of Church support against individual delinquents, by a refusal of Sacramental absolution or the denial of other Sacraments, must appear not only rash and imprudent, but practically forbidden. There is no doubt, however, that ordinaries have the power to enforce the precept,[57] especially if a certain definite contribution has been prescribed. The Holy See has sometimes instructed them to avail themselves of this power and compel their subjects to do their duty. Alexander III wrote to the Archbishop of Canterbury and his suffragans, as follows:

> Mandamus, quatenus parochianos vestros monere curetis, et si opus fuerit, sub excommunicationis districtione compellere, ut de lana decimas ecclesiis, quibus debentur, omni contradictione et appellatione cessante, cum integritate persolvant.[58]

3.—Sanctions

According to the present legislation, the Ordinary could employ canon 2222 in proceeding against grave and notorious delinquents.[59] If the guilty party had been repeatedly admonished he could even inflict censures.[60] The following would seem to offer a good method of procedure, if the ordinary should find it necessary to act.

> Catholics flagrantly neglecting their duties are in the first instance to be kindly admonished by their pastor: if this is not heeded, the pastor will admonish them before some trustworthy witness. In case this second admonition fails, their names are to be sent to the chancery office, together with the facts in the case,

---

[56] S. C. de Prop. Fide, 13 Maii, 1816, n. 4—*Coll.*, n. 713.
[57] Cappello, *De Visitatione*, II, 629-630.
[58] C. 5, X, *De Decimis, Primitiis et Oblationibus*, III, 30; cf. also c. 32, *loc. cit.*, and C. Trid., sess. XXI, *de ref.*, c. 4.
[59] Haring, "Ueber kirchliche Abgaben," *LQS*, LXXVIII (1925), 343.
[60] Can. 2222.

> to be made the basis of any necessary proceeding. Catholics obstinately refusing to comply with their parochial duties, upon conviction, may be partially or wholly refused the privileges of the Church by the ordinary.[61]

This, or some similar method of proceeding against a gravely guilty delinquent, has the advantages of preventing undue haste in condemning him, of permitting greater impartiality of judgment as to the gravity of the guilt, and of offering a greater probability of reform, since the interposition of the higher superior is more likely to impress the guilty party with the gravity of his fault. Prudence would, however, dictate that the pastor confer with the ordinary, even before proceeding to the first formal admonition, and act throughout with the greatest charity and circumspection, lest the delinquent suspect that the pastor may be acting because of some personal animus.

Whether it is ever advisable to resort to such methods depends on a great number of possible circumstances, and must be left to the judgment of the clergy concerned. Conditions may arise when the common welfare will demand that, when moral suasion has proven insufficient, some stronger measures be resorted to in order to prevent greater harm because of scandal. The Church, however, does not favor compulsion. A review of the legislation of the Code, in regard to Church support, combined with the total abrogation of all penalties for refusal, leaves the impression that it is far more in accord with the spirit of the Church to appeal to the good will of the faithful to obtain the necessary means, rather than to compel contributions.[62]

What penalties are to be employed, should the ordinary find it necessary to resort to force, is a troublesome question. It is apparent that if the delinquent is gravely guilty and obstinate, Sacramental absolution would have to be denied to him, just as to any other unrepentant grave sin-

---

[61] Synodal Decrees of the Diocese of St. Cloud (1924), n. 81-82; cf. also the Diocesan Statutes of Harrisburg (1928), n. 367, for a similar mode of procedure.

[62] Cf. Haring, "Ueber kirchliche Abgaben," *LQS*, LXXVIII (1925), 343.

ner. But to be morally certain of the presence of grave guilt is generally impossible in actual life, if the rules set down by Kenrick are to serve as a norm. And if there is doubt about the gravity of the guilt, the confessor would have to give the penitent the benefit of the doubt and absolve him. Under these circumstances, the infliction of the graver penalties, excommunication and interdict, would certainly be unjustified.[63]

The policy of the French Episcopate, after the separation from the State in 1904, might be worthy of study. At that time the French Church suddenly found herself deprived of her former sources of support and obliged to depend entirely upon the donations of the people. As a sanction, to enforce the duty of support, two kinds of penalties were decided upon; one which was to be inflicted upon the parish, and the other upon individuals. If a parish would refuse to contribute its proportionate share to the general fund, which was to be raised for the benefit of the entire French Church, it was to be lowered to the grade of a filial parish, or, in extreme cases, the clergy were to be withdrawn and the parish left without any services, a penalty equivalent to temporary suppression. Individual delinquents were to forfeit the right to all external solemnity in connection with the reception of the Sacraments and other spiritual ministrations.[64]

Of how much value such penalties might be in our country would remain to be seen. It is hardly probable that in this country the virtual suppression of a parish would be as effectual a threat as it might be in a country where the parish, with all its local traditions and associations, is so closely interwoven with the life of the people. In such a country even the indifferent Catholics might be aroused to contribute in order to prevent the infliction of such a shame upon their community. In this country, on the contrary, the closing of a church might possibly be regarded in the

---

[63] Can. 2218, §2.

[64] Platz, *Geistige Kämpfe im modernen Frankreich*, p. 493; cf. also Haring, "Ueber kirchliche Abgaben," *LQS*, LXXVIII (1925), 336; and Abbé Dimnet, "The Church in France, Its Present Position," *Dublin Review*, CXXXVIII (1906), 177-179.

light of a hidden blessing by many parishioners, since it freed them from a financial burden. Local traditions and local pride would not have much influence, as most parishes are too young and the population too shifting. Instead of working for the reopening of their own church, many of these parishioners would casually drop in at Sunday Mass at some neighboring church, without bothering about joining the parish, and, in the meanwhile, calmly await further developments. The refusal of external solemnities might be treated in the same manner. Caution would have to be used in the infliction of such quasi-penalties lest the authorities lay themselves open to ridicule.

Moral suasion can, however, often be used with great effect. Such practices as the public acknowledgment of substantial donations, the expression of public thanks, and the public recitation of prayers for all the benefactors of the parish, the printing and distribution of annual reports, indicating how much each parishioner contributed during the past year, will generally prove of value. Besides, the development of parish spirit and loyalty, and the fostering of parish societies, even of such as are not intended to be of direct service in financial matters, will prove materially beneficial. But all of these means can be used only in places where the population is stationary to some degree. The pastor of a church, where most of the worshippers are "floaters" and transients, will always have to depend either upon his own ingenuity in inducing these people to contribute or upon diocesan support, or, a possibility of the future, upon some endowment, for the necessary funds to enable him to remain solvent.

4.—Methods of Fulfilling the Obligation

In connection with this the question might be raised as to which system is preferable, support from the State, from endowments, from enforced contributions such as the tithes, or dependence upon the voluntary contributions of the people. Each system has its advantages and disadvantages. The first two systems guarantee a relatively certain and constant revenue. The pastor need not devote himself to the raising of the necessary funds, and will have more time and energy to attend to the spiritual affairs of his parishioners. Announcements about financial matters and the dreaded money sermons can be dispensed with.

A danger of these systems lies in the fact that such financial independence of the Church may tend to bring about an alienation between the lay people and the clergy. Unless the clergy is exceptionally sincere and zealous, the inclination will show itself to keep aloof from the faithful, to discharge their duties in a somewhat routine way, respond to any calls that may be made upon them for their services, but, outside of this, to lose interest in and contact with their people. This aloofness, and the resulting indifference of the people towards the Church, is often mentioned as one of the chief causes that helped to bring on the Reformation and the French Revolution.[65]

State support also has the disadvantage of offering the civil government an opportunity of interfering in ecclesiastical affairs.[66] Even if the concessions made to the State as a return for its financial aid have been accurately fixed, e.g., by a Concordat, there is always the possibility, as experience has demonstrated, that the State will overstep these bounds or will use the powers granted to it in an unforeseen way, almost always to the detriment of the Church. Should the ecclesiastical authorities object, the State can enforce its pretensions by threatening to withdraw its support. And, unless it be a matter of principle, where the Church must resist, she will generally yield to prevent the disturbances arising from a sudden and radical change in the system of support.

During the Middle Ages the Church persistently refused to accept a salary from the State for her clergy, because, as Honorius III replied to such an offer from Hugh, King of Cyprus, it would endanger her liberty.[67] It was also because of this danger of interference from the State that

---

[65] Kurth-Day, *The Church At the Turning Points of History*, p. 165.

[66] To realize the lengths to which the State may go in its interference in Church affairs, cf. Kurth-Day, *op. cit.*, p. 59 et seq.; also Alzog, *Man. of Univ. Ch. Hist.*, II, 340, footnote.

[67] Alzog, *op. cit.*, II, 651.

the "Irish bishops unanimously declined the endowment offered by the government in 1837, preferring to remain poor but free." [68] One of the advantages of the separation of 1905 in France was the removal of the following restrictions, to which the Church had been forced to subject herself, unless she preferred to break off relations with the State. "No Papal letter could be promulgated without the knowledge and sanction of government, no meeting of bishops could take place without a special permission, no bishop could stir from the limits of his diocese without giving due notice to the Minister of Cults." Practically all the beneficiaries "were appointed by agreement with the minister; and this meant, in most cases, especially in the last thirty years, that they were appointed by the minister alone, the Papal Nuncio offering more or less resistance. The *conseils de fabrique* or Church boards had never enjoyed absolute freedom, the mayor being a member of them by right of office; and since 1895 their accounts were looked into by the inspectors of finance, and the parish income was carefully checked and submitted to special regulations." [69] These concessions to the State, which had been forced into the Concordat by Napoleon I, are, indeed, far wider than those usually granted by the Holy See, but they serve to show how the State, if it should become hostile or even only over-officious, can hamper the Church in her liberty of action and usefulness. Practically all the French bishops concurred that the separation, which abolished these concessions, "had been beneficial to the Church from the spiritual point of view." [70]

Endowments, especially if they become very large, will also tend to arouse the envy of non-Catholics, and may tempt the civil government, even though it claims to be Catholic, to look for pretexts to confiscate these endow-

---

[68] Alzog, *op. cit.*, III, 737.

[69] Abbé Dimnet, "The Church in France, Its Present Position," *Dublin Review*, CXXXVIII (1906), 177.

[70] Boyd, "The French Ecclesiastical Revolution," *Am. Cath. Quart. Rev.*, XXXII (1907), p. 647; cf. also *Raccolta di Concordati*, "Pace Fra Innocenzo VIII e Ferdinando di Napoli, 1492, p. 223-225, for other examples of how the State can interfere with the Church's activity.

ments.[71] One of the chief factors which helped to spread and consolidate the Reformation movement was the desire of the nobility to enrich themselves by looting the endowments and properties of the Church. The fact that they would be compelled to restore this loot made them resort to all possible measures to prevent the reestablishment of the Catholic faith. To justify the persecutions to which the Catholics were subjected in the effort to destroy the Church's last hope of recovering the ground which she had lost, the most amazing calumnies were spread against the Church with such persistence and thoroughness that they have persisted to the present day.[72] All this was done to enable those who had been enriched at the expense of the Church to retain these riches. Had it not been for this, the Protestant revolt might have quickly died out.[73]

Large endowments may also induce individuals to enter the clerical state, not because of any spiritual motives, but because of the temporal benefits which they hope to enjoy.[74] And even if this should not be true, the faithful may, nevertheless, suspect that clerics were led to enter the clerical state for some such motive. Experience shows that these dangers are actually connected with large endowments.

Dependence on voluntary contributions also has certain defects to counterbalance its advantages. As has already been mentioned, this system frequently compels the clergy to devote too much time and energy, which might be better employed otherwise, in devising ways and means for the gathering of the necessary funds. Such continual absorp-

---

[71] Kurth-Day, *The Church At the Turning Points of History*, p. 103 et seq.; Pöschl, "Die Entstehung des geistlichen Beneficiums," *AkKR*, CVI (1926), 59-60; Alzog, *op. cit.*, III, 676, 861 and 955; *Raccolta di Concordati*, pp. 36-37 and 63; Vogt, *Das kirchliche Vermögensrecht*, pp. 41-42; MacCaffrey, *History of the Church from the Renaissance to the Reformation*, I, 124 and 130; Donat Sampson, "Pius VI and the French Revolution," *Am. Cath. Quart. Rev.*, XXXI (1906), 222-225, 229, 431 and 435.

[72] Cf. Vernon Johnson, *One Lord, One Faith*, pp. 43, 50, 114, 155, 203, etc., for indications of the enduring influence of these calumnies.

[73] Cf. Belloc, *How the Reformation Happened*, for a further exposition of this view.

[74] Kurth-Day, *The Church At the Turning Points of History*, pp. 58-63; also Creighton, *History of the Papacy During the Reformation*, I, 308.

tion in financial affairs must inevitably threaten to weaken the spiritual life of one who finds himself continually faced with the problem of how to keep his parish, or the institutions for which he is responsible, solvent, because of the apathetic response of the people to whom he must appeal for help.[75] That some of those who find themselves in such discouraging circumstances should become bitter and misanthropic, is not surprising. And such a lowering of the spiritual morale of the clergy must inevitably have a baneful effect upon the people. These dangers will, however, decrease, as the Church slowly advances beyond the "building age," with the consequent decrease of extraordinary expenses.

Voluntary Church support, however, also has its advantages. According to the old adage that a man loves anything in proportion to the sacrifices which he makes for it, the faithful will be more interested in the welfare of their church if it has been built and is supported by their own personal contributions. They feel more closely united with the Church, and so come more completely under her influence. As a consequence of this, and of the graces which they will receive in return for their generosity towards religion, they will also benefit spiritually.

The clergy will also be more closely united with their people, as they will have to depend upon them for their support. There will not be so much danger that a feeling of superiority will make them keep aloof, or lead them to treat their parishioners with indifference. The development of a feeling of dependence has always been recommended as a powerful help to foster the spirit of humility and meekness. And often, since they are but human, and human motives will always have their influence, the fact that they are dependent on their flock for their own support and for the funds they need to conduct their parochial

[75] Numerous examples of extraordinary methods resorted to by some of the clergy, at various times, can be found in Shea, *The Catholic Church in the United States*. Thus, in 1803, Bishop Carroll gave permission that a great lottery be held to help defray the expenses of building the Cathedral of Baltimore, cf. Shea, *op. cit.*, II, 600. That the employment of such desperate means cannot benefit the spiritual life of either the clergy or the faithful seems clear.

activities will urge them to make greater efforts to draw back into the Church such as are becoming indifferent, in order to lighten their own financial cares by obtaining a greater number of contributors.

What would seem to be the ideal solution for the problem of Church support in the United States? That the Church is in favor of voluntary support has already been mentioned. Dependence on voluntary support is not to be considered the last desperate expedient when other means of support are wanting, but, rather, the traditional policy of the Church. Pöschl [76] says that the Church has been able, as a general rule, to rely on the generosity of the faithful, and that compulsory systems of taxation, such as the tithes, have been the exceptional means resorted to because of extraordinary circumstances. During the very century when compulsory support was most widely introduced by the laws of Charlemagne, who enforced the payment of tithes by everybody, this settled conviction of the Church, that voluntary support is the ideal method of support, was again clearly enunciated in the Council of Châlon.

> Animarum quippe salutem inquirere sacerdos, non lucra terrena, debet: quoniam fideles ad res suas dandas non sunt cogendi, neque circumveniendi. Oblatio enim spontanea esse debet, juxta id quod ait Scriptura: Voluntarie sacrificabo tibi, et illud: Omnis populus mente devota obtulerunt donaria Domino.[77]

Pius X, therefore, was not urging anything new and untried upon the French bishops when he advised them,[78] in 1904, to appeal for voluntary contributions, saying that coercive measures were not compatible with the spirit of the Church. The generosity of the present-day Catholic has again vindicated the faith of the Church. The French Church offers a splendid example. Through the Separation she lost all her endowments, which had produced a revenue of about a hundred million dollars.[79] Appeals to the gen-

[76] "Die Entstehung des geistlichen Beneficiums," *AkKR*, CVI (1926), 40.

[77] C. Cabilonense II (813), c. 6—*Mansi*, XIV, 94-95.

[78] Selinger, "The Theory and Practice of Church Revenue," *American Eccl. Rev.*, LXII (1920), 673.

[79] Boyd, "The French Ecclesiastical Revolution," *Am. Cath. Quart. Rev.*, XXXII (1907), 648.

erosity of the faithful met with such a hearty response that not only were these losses offset, but the Church was enabled to maintain Catholic schools all over France.[80] This generosity was displayed by a people who have often been accused of being Catholics only in name, Catholics, not because of conviction, but because tradition, combined with indifference to religion in general, prevented them from making the effort of breaking with the Church.

The Catholics of other countries are equally generous. In Ireland the people have always contributed generously,[81] even during the time when they had to pay the full tithes for the support of the established Anglican Church.[82] The faithful in England have drawn especial praise from a non-Catholic author for their energy and willingness to make sacrifices.[83]

In spite of occasional complaints,[84] the Catholics of the United States have generally distinguished themselves for their spirit of sacrifice. The rapidity with which churches and Catholic institutions of all kinds were being built, "by the spontaneous offerings of those who in most cases were manfully struggling to secure a livelihood or modest competence," [85] was startling to those outside the Church.[86] The best proof of their willingness to make sacrifices for their religion is to be found in the steadily increasing number of Catholic schools and colleges, all built and maintained by their voluntary offerings. All this is proof positive that the Church can still continue to trust in the generosity of her children to provide the necessary means.

---

[80] Gwynn, Denis, "For the Good Name of France," *The Commonweal*, IX (1929), 384.

[81] Alzog, *Man. of Univ. Ch. Hist.*, III, 737.

[82] Alzog, *op. cit.*, III, 858; cf. also Llandaff, "An Irish Election," *Dublin Review*, CXXXVIII (1906), 28.

[83] Cf. Review of "Life and Labor of the People in London," by Chas. Booth, *Dublin Review*, CXXXVI (1905), 232.

[84] Maes, *Life of Father Nerinckx*, pp. 87 and 92; Shea, *op. cit.*, III, 277 and 295; Webb, *Centenary of Catholicity in Kentucky*, p. 166; Fitton, *Sketch of the Establishment of the Church in New England*, p. 161.

[85] Shea, *op. cit.*, II, 678.

[86] Beard, *The Rise of American Civilization*, II, 397 and 409.

At the same time, however, the Church has always acted on the presumption that absolute dependence on voluntary contributions, to provide for all her needs, is somewhat too precarious a situation. Thus in the Gregorian Decretals [87] the rule was laid down: "Sancitum est, ut unicuique ecclesiae unus mansus integer absque ullo servitio tribuatur." Practically all her legislation, before the existing Code, was based on the supposition that each benefice had some revenue-bearing property, or some other certain income, such as State support or tithes, attached to it.[88] Voluntary contributions alone were not considered to be certain enough to constitute an endowment for a benefice. It is true that the new legislation has changed this rule, so that *"certae et voluntariae fidelium oblationes, quae ad beneficii rectorem spectant,"* [89] are sufficient to constitute the *dos beneficii*, and the Church no longer insists on anything more than this. That she still prefers some more certain and stable source of revenue, at least for certain purposes, is apparent from the tenor of the common law.[90]

A combination of these two systems, i.e., the formation of endowments for the maintenance of certain activities, and dependence on voluntary contributions for others, seems to be the closest approximation to the ideal, and also practicable in this country. The ordinary parish which has, for the greater part, stable members, can and will have to depend on the generosity of these members. It is true that some parishes have an endowment, or are gradually accumulating one. But the overwhelming majority will not find this possible for many years to come.

For the support of certain activities of the Church, for the maintenance of the charitable and educational institutions, possibly also the diocesan curias, the gradual formation of endowment funds seems to offer the best solution.[91] This is especially true in regard to higher schools, as it is

[87] C. 1, X, *De Censibus, Exactionibus et Procurationibus*, III, 39.

[88] Vermeersch-Creusen, *Epitome, I. C.*, II, n. 743; Augustine, *Commentary*, VI, 493 et seq.

[89] Can. 1410.

[90] Haring, "Ueber kirchliche Abgaben," *LQS*, LXXVIII (1925), 337; cf. also Can. 1489, §2.

[91] Cf. Conc. Plen. Balt. III, n. 211.

difficult to convince the common faithful that they should help support these institutions. The general attitude is that those who benefit directly from these schools should be willing to support them. Special collections for educational purposes, therefore, are not very popular nor satisfactory, as they help to swell the continued drain from the parish funds for outside activities.

> If the pastor is obliged to send too much money out of the congregation to support diocesan, national and international worthy charities, and if he cannot show a financial improvement in his parish affairs, the people who see only what is in their midst, and not the other outside activities, will become discouraged and tighten their purse-strings so that it will become impossible to meet the local situation.[92]

It is fortunate, for Catholic higher education in America, that the various religious bodies have maintained these colleges with their customary self-sacrifice and zeal, covering the deficits, due to the low tuition, with funds obtained from other sources. The formation of substantial endowments seems, therefore, necessary for a permanent solution of the problem of supporting the educational institutions,[93] and it is an encouraging feature in the American Church that these endowments, due to the generosity of the faithful, are gradually accumulating.[94]

5.—*Extent of the Obligation*

How much may the faithful be expected to give? Should they be asked for a certain fixed sum, or for a certain proportion of their income? Schmalzgrueber [95] says that some

---

[92] Jansen, "Church Support," *Homil. and Past. Rev.*, XXVIII (1927), 268.

[93] Blakely, "The Educational Year," *America*, XXXVIII (1927), 296.

[94] In 1926 reports from 113 Catholic colleges showed that 39 of these had endowments totaling $17,402,217.—Blakely, *loc. cit.* *The Official Catholic Year Book*, 1928, pp. 30-32, lists the larger donations which were made to the Church during the year from August, 1927, to August, 1928. The total was in excess of nine million, a great part of which, no doubt, helped to swell various endowments. Drives for endowments, scholarships, etc., are being conducted continually, generally with good success.

[95] *Ius Ecclesiasticum Universum*, III, 48, 63.

maintain that an equal amount should be asked of each individual, whether he be rich or poor, because each one obtains the same benefit from the Church. He, however,[96] holds the opinion of those who say that each one is to contribute according to his means. The author is here treating of the question as to who should contribute towards the building and repairing of churches. But the same arguments apply when there is question of apportioning the contributions for the other needs of the Church.

The latter opinion appears to be the juster and more in accord with the spirit of the Church. It is, indeed, theoretically true that everybody obtains the same benefits from the services of the Church. But to actually receive these benefits, the same amount of sacrifice is presupposed of each one. If every parishioner is to contribute an equal amount, the sacrifice will not be equal. The payment of a specified sum may represent an actual diminution of the comforts of life for the poorer members of the parish, while, for the richer, it will be altogether inconsequential.

Neither is the "one-price system" [97] in accord with the spirit of Christianity. From the very beginning the duty of all to contribute according to their means was fully recognized [98] and carried into practice in the tithing system. The contributing of an amount proportioned to their wealth is also enjoined again and again upon the faithful in the legislation of the Church.[99]

What this proportion should be will depend upon the needs of the parish and of the diocese. In some dioceses a definite proportion has been specified, the payment of which will give the donor the full assurance that he has

---

[96] *Op. cit.*, III, 48, 64.

[97] Cf. Menge, "A Substitute for Pew Rent," *Am. Eccl. Rev.*, LXII (1920), 462-467; also Sans Souci, "Weekly Envelope Collections," *Am. Eccl. Rev.*, LXII (1920), 577-580.

[98] Gasquet, *Parish Life in Medieval England*, p. 5.

[99] Thus in this country: Syn. Dioec. Balt. I (1791), n. 23—*Coll. Lac.*, III, 6; Conc. Plen. Balt. III, Pastoral Letter of Dec. 7th, 1884, under "Education of the Clergy"; Dioc. Stat. of St. Louis (1929), n. 161; Dioc. Stat. of Buffalo (1927), art. 495; Dioc. Stat. of Harrisburg (1928), n. 367.

done his duty in this respect.[100] Thus in Seattle[101] and in St. Cloud[102] four per cent of the gross income has been designated as an equitable proportion to be devoted to works of religion. In Superior[103] the faithful are asked to contribute five per cent, and in Cincinnati,[104] from seven to ten per cent. In some places the contributions of one day's earnings each month is urged, while in Des Moines[105] an effort is being made to reintroduce the full tithes.

It is sometimes objected that it is preposterous to expect Catholics to pay full tithes; that the modern conditions of life preclude the possibility of people donating one-tenth of their income to religion, since the average individual does not and cannot save one-tenth of his income, or anything approximating that amount. To expect him to pay tithes would, therefore, be asking him to do what is practically impossible. Actual experience, however, shows that it is possible. In 1920, 210,000 members of the Methodist sect agreed to pay the full tithes.[106] Various religious bodies, such as the Mormons[107] and the Seventh Day Adventists,[108] demand that all their members pay the tithes. Whether it is advisable to impose such a burden upon the faithful, unless the Church is in absolute need of that percentage of the income of its members, may be questioned.

Where the Church's income is not sufficient for her needs, instead of asking the individuals to make larger donations, in most cases it might be more successful, and certainly more equitable, if an effort were made to induce a larger proportion of the faithful to contribute. According to the

---

100 Regarding the advisability of determining the percentage of their income, which the faithful are expected to contribute to the Church, cf. Chap. III, under "Assessments."

101 Jansen, "Church Support," *Hom. and Past. Rev.*, XXVIII (1927), p. 268.

102 Synodal Decrees of the Diocese of St. Cloud (1924), n. 79.

103 Based on the oral statement of a pastor of that diocese.

104 Also based on the oral statement of a priest of that diocese.

105 Jansen, *op. cit.*, p. 268.

106 Noll, "A Talk on Parish Finance," *The Acolyte*, IV (1928), n. 1, p. 6.

107 U. S. Dept. of Commerce, Bureau of the Census, *Religious Bodies*, II, 676.

108 *Op. cit.*, II, 26.

general opinion, only about one-half of the faithful support the Church.[109] If a respectable number of these delinquents could be reached and persuaded to contribute, most of the pressing financial difficulties would be disposed of. But before expecting to attain this result, the pastor would have to determine the reasons for the existence of such a regrettable condition in his particular parish.

Many factors have concurred in bringing about such a state of affairs. The most common are:

1. The fact that a large number of people have no permanent residence. Due to the fact that they have no permanent means of support in any one place, or because they expect to find better opportunities, better home conditions or cheaper rent, or, merely because of their nomadic instincts, very many are continually moving. As long as this tendency to drift from place to place remains, this factor will always present a problem. The parochial clergy may find it possible to overcome it, to some extent, by continual exertion in locating these new parishioners. But even with the best of intentions, they will often find themselves unable to cope with this problem. The introduction of the lay apostolate might prove very beneficial in these circumstances. Besides helping to keep these people who are continually moving more closely united to the Church, which must always be their chief purpose, they would also incidentally help solve the problem of support by inducing them to contribute.

2. The lack of personal contact between the laity and the clergy, especially in the larger parishes, where the individual is often lost in the multitudes. The remedies mentioned above would also prove serviceable in combating this condition.

3. The difficulty with which many immigrants readjust themselves to the financial condition of the Church in this country. In their native land they were accustomed to a well-endowed Church which, instead of having to appeal for support from the faithful, was able to help the needy from

---

[109] Noll, "The Practical Way of Supporting Religion," *Amer. Eccl. Rev.*, LXII (1920), 273.

her own revenues. Instruction, tact and zealous charity will do wonders under these circumstances.[110]

4. Ignorance or carelessness, as to the binding force of the obligation of Church support. Instruction and a better education, especially of the children, will help to overcome this trouble, to some extent.

5. Suspicions that the income of the Church is more than sufficient for her needs, that she squanders her resources on useless objects or activities, or that the clergy is enriching itself at the expense of the laity. In many cases such suspicions merely serve as an excuse for shirking the obligation of supporting the Church. Where they do not, they may be met by the publication of a detailed and accurate report of the receipts and expenditures of the parish or institution in question.

6. The introduction of national feelings and prejudices. Pastors, descended from a different nationality than that of most of their parishioners, frequently have to contend with the disapproval or even antagonism of their flock. The refusal to recognize national distinctions within the Church, and the display of true priestly spirit in life and action will enable the pastor to obtain the respect and support of his people. In time, as the national lines gradually disappear, this difficulty will also pass. Parishioners of different races may sometimes refuse to co-operate, or the old parishioners may be slow to welcome new members from another race, or even ostracise them. Until the differences of descent are forgotten, pastors can do much to render them harmless by their own good will and charity.

7. Personal enmity against the clergy connected with the parish. This difficulty can only be attacked by removal of the reasons, whatever they be, for this animosity, or the removal of the clerics concerned, to a more productive field of labor.

8. Indifference to religion in general. The patent and only cure for this is the conversion of the persons concerned.

---

[110] Bandini, "Concerning the Italian Problem," *Amer. Eccl. Rev.*, LXII (1920), 278-285.

CHAPTER THREE

Methods of Support

One of the most striking features of Church support in the United States is the utter lack of uniformity in the obtaining of the necessary income. Except for the fact that they are all voluntary, at least in principle, the various ways in which the contributions of the faithful are obtained in different communities, or even in different churches in the same community, are often so dissimilar as to shock casual worshippers. A person who in his own community has always been accustomed to see an elderly usher pass quietly through the aisles, and, with a dignified little gesture of acknowledgment, extend the collection plate to those who wished to contribute, is very likely to be disedified by his first experience in a church where a corps of business-like young men move from pew to pew and ask each seat-holder for a specified donation, instantly ready to return the proper change should a larger sum be proffered. What the results would be if this same person, after having invited a curious non-Catholic friend to accompany him, should happen to enter a church where the door-collection is taken up, and where the money tables and signs indicating how much each is expected to give are prominent fixtures in the vestibule, can only be left to the imagination. That his equanimity would, at the very least, be disturbed, cannot be doubted.

It is regrettable that such conditions exist; that the question of Church support should be an occasion of scandal to even a single individual. And it is just as regrettable that, owing to a variety of circumstances, this state of affairs is unavoidable. The parochial clergy of the United States has always been forced to struggle with the problem of inducing peoples of widely different nationalities and mentalities to practice their common religion, and support it with at least some degree of harmony. They have had to coax or bully contributions out of people who, having always been accustomed to give, give freely; from people who having long been without the services of religion, because they lived in a new or sparsely settled territory, had forgotten that they were expected to give; from people who, being immigrants from countries where the Church did not need their contributions, could not understand why they should now be obliged to give; and even from people who, unlearned and suspicious of everyone in their new home, feared that they were being imposed upon by a pastor of another nationality, and were, therefore, unwilling to give. From all these various kinds of worshippers, most of them poor, their pastors had to obtain sufficient funds, not only to support the work of religion, but often to build up from the very foundations the entire material structure of the Church. It is not surprising, therefore, that all possible methods of raising funds were brought into play, and that occasionally, in sheer desperation, fantastic and even questionable schemes for increasing the revenues were resorted to. To know all may not always mean to forgive all. But to know all, or even a part, of the problem of Church support which the American clergy had and still has to cope with, will mean, in almost all cases, to condone much, if not all.

The various methods of Church support that are more or less in use in this country can be divided into four groups:

1. Support from endowments.

2. Those methods which may be called quasi-compulsory, the amount to be contributed being determined for the different individuals, at least to some extent, so that the power of public opinion may be brought to bear upon the contributors to urge payment. The chief ones are: assessments, pew rents, seat-money collections, and door-collections.

3. Those methods which are purely voluntary, and where the amount to be given is left entirely to the free will of the contributor. Such are the offertory collection, free will donations and legacies.

4. Those methods which may be called extraordinary, and which may be voluntary or, to some extent, compulsory. They are extraordinary because they are hardly ever intended to be the main source of revenues, but merely serve to augment the general fund, or to provide for some special needs. Of these the number is legion.

1.—Endowments.

As has already been mentioned, the endowing of certain extra-parochial activities of the Church, such as the diocesan curia and the educational and charitable institutions, appears to be the best solution of the problem of their support. The annual assessing of the parishes, or the taking up of collections, absolutely necessary under present conditions for the maintenance of these branches of the Church's activity, but often a continual source of irritation or of financial embarrassment for the parishes, could then be dispensed with. That the Church favors the establishment of such endowments is sufficiently proven by her common law. Although she no longer grants the right of patronage to persons who make a notable donation to some benefice,[1] she, however, permits the ordinary to give certain privileges to such benefactors, as a return for their liberality.

Canon 1450.—§2. Loci autem Ordinarius potest:

1°. Fidelibus qui ex toto vel ex parte ecclesias exstruxerint vel beneficia fundaverint, spiritualia suffragia, eorum liberalitati proportionata, concedere vel ad tempus vel etiam in perpetuum;

2°. Fundationem beneficii admittere ea adiecta conditione, ut beneficium prima vice conferatur clerico fundatori vel alii clerico a fundatore designato.

If wealthy Catholics were sometimes informed of this provision of the Church, they might be more inclined to make such liberal contributions. The knowledge that the supreme authority of the Church has placed this stamp of approval upon such liberality will often prove a greater

---

[1] Can. 1450, §1.

inducement than the promises of lower members of the hierarchy.

Such substantial donations by individuals will, however, always be comparatively rare. If adequate numbers of endowments are to be established, other means will have to be employed also. The Church has, and explicitly claims, the right to acquire temporal goods by all just means, which are permitted to other persons by natural or divine law.[2] There need, therefore, be no hesitancy in using some of the methods which have been evolved in recent years, as long as they are just. Other methods which have been employed in the past to build up endowments should also be encouraged.

In former centuries, in accordance with a praiseworthy custom, the Church was made a beneficiary in practically all last wills.[3] This pious practice has fallen into sad neglect, especially in this country.[4] This may be due, in part, to the business-like way in which testamentary concerns are disposed of, as if they were mere commercial transactions, into which no thought of anything spiritual is permitted to intrude. The clergy, however, can accomplish much towards the reestablishment of the old Catholic conception, according to which a testament was considered as the last account which the individual gave of his stewardship of the temporal goods entrusted to him by God. Instead of being oversensitive, and scrupulously avoiding all references to testamentary affairs, or feeling embarrassed and apologetic when, as occasionally happens, a will is published in which the Church has been remembered, because they fear that the Church will be accused of abusing her privileged position at the bedside of the dying, they should bring this matter to the attention of the faithful and praise those who remember the Church. There is no need of

---

[2] Can. 1499, §1.

[3] Gasquet, *Parish Life in Medieval England*, p. 133: "The practice of leaving sums of money by will to the [Church] wardens for definite purposes, was almost universal in the last half of the 15th century." Cf. also Doheny, *Church Property, Modes of Acquisition*, pp. 84 and 88.

[4] Donovan, "Catholic Clannishness," *The Commonweal*, XI (1930), 736.

abolishing a good custom, because it has been abused occasionally to the serious detriment of the testator's family. The natural law suggests, indeed, that suitable provision should be made for the family.[5] It does not demand, however, that they be made the heirs of the entire estate.

In her common law [6] the Church mentions legacies as one mode by which she can acquire property, and prescribes how such legacies are to be administered. She did not consider it necessary to recommend such pious bequests explicitly in her common law, because her approval is sufficiently evident from past legislation.[7] Thus the First Provincial Council of Halifax advised the clergy to urge the people to make such bequests.[8]

> Hortetur sacerdos aegrotum...temporalia sua disponere,...atque pauperibus vel piis usibus providere si facultates suae hoc permittant, ut peccata sua eleemosynis redimens et amicos faciens de mammona iniquitatis, recipiatur ab eis in aeterna tabernacula.

The First Provincial Council of Westminster also recommended such bequests, warning the priest, however, to be prudent lest he be suspected of avarice.

> Cavendum est ne sacerdos in aliquam incidat avaritiae suspicionem, se testamentorum confectioni immiscens, si saltem in commodum ecclesiae vel pauperum bonorum partem moribundus cedat. Sed ab insanis quorumdam clamoribus non deterreatur ab officio...eos hortandi qui nunquam in pauperes misericordiam fecerunt, ut tandem aliquando peccata sua eleemosynis redimant.[9]

Pastors and other instructors of the faithful are to be commended, therefore, if they advise their charges to remember the Church in their wills. In the sickroom itself it may be better to be too prudent rather than too insistent regarding this matter. But they can mention it very opportunely in the ordinary course of instructions or sermons

---

[5] Schmalzgrueber, *Ius Ecclesiasticum Universum*, III, 26, 1, 7.
[6] Canons 1513-1517.
[7] Cf. Doheny, *Church Property, Modes of Acquisition*, pp. 88 and 89.
[8] Conc. Prov. Halifax. I (1857), XV, 4—*Coll. Lac.*, III, 746.
[9] Conc. Prov. Westm. I (1852), XXV, 8—*Coll. Lac.*, III, 942.

when they speak of the advisability of putting worldly affairs in order so that they may not prove a source of distraction and worry when the person finds himself in danger of death. By such repeated reminders Catholics may be induced to reestablish this beautiful custom, so that testaments in which religion is remembered will no longer be the exception, but the general rule. The revenues from these bequests would be an appreciable assistance in the formation of endowments.

Another method of endowing institutions, which is in actual use, consists in imposing a tax upon each parish for this purpose, the size and wealth of the parish determining the amount of the tax. Frequently drives are instituted to raise necessary funds. A special effort is made to acquaint the faithful with the needs of the institution to be endowed, and the funds are then obtained in one of various ways. A collection may be ordered for one or more Sundays or holydays for this special purpose. Or solicitors may go from family to family asking each one for their contribution. Or again, especially where there is question of an extra-diocesan institution, appeals may be sent through the mails. All these methods have been used, generally with good results. If the faithful can be convinced that the need is a legitimate one, a generous response may be depended upon.

Another method which is becoming increasingly popular All these methods have been used, generally with good religious societies and missionary organizations experimented with this method. When it proved successful, it was quickly adopted by other agencies, so that now dioceses, educational and charitable institutions, and even parishes, are issuing these bonds.[10]

The plan as generally adopted is as follows. The donor gives a specified sum of money to the society or institution which issues these bonds. The latter agrees to pay the donor a certain rate of interest, usually five or six per cent annually, for the remainder of his life. When the donor dies the principal belongs to the society. Since loans to the Catholic Church have a justified reputation for safety, this

[10] Leaver, "Modified Annuities," *The Acolyte*, VI (1930), n. 1, p. 7.

form of investment has a special appeal for older people who wish to insure for themselves a safe income for the rest of their life. This is guaranteed to them. At the same time they have the consolation of knowing that they are helping support their religion. Without doubt, the annuity plan will become a considerable source of income for the Church, and may be used to great advantage for the establishment of endowments.

Various other methods are continually being tested; life insurance, with the Church named as the beneficiary; investment in properties that are expected to increase notably in value; the buying of stocks, generally with the futile hope of large returns, etc. These methods that have been mentioned are sufficient to indicate that endowments can, and undoubtedly will, be accumulated by other means than through direct appeals for donations for this specific purpose.

2.—Quasi-Compulsory Methods of Support

A.—The Renting of Pews

Among the quasi-compulsory methods of supporting the Church, the pew-rent system is, without doubt, one of the most widely known and practiced in our country. As a source of revenue it is a comparatively new establishment, considering the age of the Church. Until the latter half of the thirteenth century, seats were not provided in churches for anybody except the clergy, the patron of the church, and the higher nobility. These seats were generally placed in the sanctuary, while the rest of the congregation stood, knelt, or, if they cared to do so, sat on the floor in the body of the church during the services.[11]

Possibly the first reference to seats for the ordinary people is to be found in the Synod of Exeter of 1287: "Statuimus quod nullus de cetero quasi proprium sedile in ecclesia valeat vindicare, nobilibus personis et ecclesiarum patronis dumtaxat exceptis." [12] The inference is that the

---

[11] Grünewald, *Die Rechtsverhältnisse an Kirchenstühlen,* p. 2.
[12] C. 12—*Mansi,* XXIV, 802.

common people were beginning to have their seats generally built by themselves. There was, however, no uniform arrangement of these seats, each person building his wherever he pleased, and of whatever size or shape he pleased.[13]

Such a state of affairs naturally gave rise to much confusion and trouble, so that the authorities found it necessary to regulate the question of seats. Pews were erected at the cost of the parish, and the seats then rented or sold, either for a stated period of time or for life. Various customs, regarding the right of him who bought a seat to rent it to another, or to pass it on to his heirs, grew up in different localities. Pews were sold outright, so that they became a part of the property of the buyer; they were rented off, or even auctioned off to the highest bidder. Finally, however, a more uniform system, according to which they were rented, sometimes for life, grew up. The right to dispose of them by bequest was, however, entirely abolished. This evolution extended from the sixteenth to the nineteenth century. The funds obtained by the renting of the pews became a very important source of income in many parishes.

The practice of renting pews is a German development, and outside of the United States has never become general in any other country, at least in Europe. Even up to the present time, pews have not been introduced as common fixtures in churches in the Latin countries. Consequently there can be no question of renting them. Instead of pews single, portable chairs are generally found, and for their use seat-money may be asked.

The renting of pews seems to have been unknown also among the early Catholics of the United States. When Bishop Carroll, in his pastoral letter of 1792, speaks of the duty of Church support, he orders that it be obtained by the taking up of the Offertory collection. No mention is made of the custom of renting pews. The first reference

---

[13] "Jeder suchte sich nach Willkür einen Platz in der Kirche und baute sich da auf seine Kosten einen Stuhl, oft so, dass, wie die Niedersächsische Kirchenordnung sagt: einer den anderen an dem Gehör göttlichen Worts und dem Gesichte nach dem Tisch des Herrn merklich verhinderte." Grünewald, *op. cit.*, p. 4, quoting Uhlhorn, *Korreferat*, p. 453.

to this practice in this country appears to be that contained in the decrees of the second diocesan synod of Philadelphia, held in May, 1842.[14] Another reference is found in the first diocesan synod of New York, which was held in August of the same year.[15] Since this custom is of Germanic origin, its introduction in these dioceses, where most of the early German immigrants settled, might be expected. From them it spread, with the growth of the Church, throughout the country, generally, however, only to those sections where large numbers of the faithful were of German descent.[16]

Only one canon is contained in the Code, which has a direct relation to the renting of pews.

Canon 1263.—§1. Potest magistratibus, pro eorum dignitate et gradu, locus in ecclesia esse distinctus, ad normam legum liturgicarum.

§2. Sine expresso Ordinarii loci consensu nemo fidelis locum habeat in ecclesia sibi suisque reservatum; Ordinarius autem consensum ne praebeat, nisi ceterorum fidelium commoditati sit sufficienter consultum.

§3. Ea semper factis in concessionibus inest tacita conditio, ut Ordinarius possit, ex iusta causa, concessionem revocare, non obstante quolibet temporis decursu.

Vermeersch-Creusen hold, indeed, that this canon has no reference to the system of pew-rent.[17] Their conclusion,

---

[14] Syn. Dioec. Phil. Secunda, n. 5.

[15] Syn. Dioec. Neo-Eboracensis Prima, n. xxviii.

[16] Among the early synods, the first diocesan synod of San Francisco (1862), n. 32, and the fourth diocesan synod of Louisville (1874), cap. III, n. 3, mention the renting of pews as a recognized source of Church income. Among the more recent, which enumerate pew-rent among the approved methods of Church support, are: First Synod of Altoona (1923), n. 134; Sixth Diocesan Synod of Boston (1919), n. 176; Eleventh Diocesan Synod of Syracuse (1922), n. 71; First Diocesan Synod of Crookston (1921), n. 404, 14; Twenty-seventh Diocesan Synod of Buffalo (1924), n. 490; Eighth Diocesan Synod of Harrisburg (1928), n. 360, 5; Fifth Diocesan Synod of Los Angeles (1927), n. 206, 1; and the Seventh Diocesan Synod of St. Louis (1929), n. 162, a.

[17] "Agitur de loco definito, v.g., de cappella quadam, non autem de sede mobili quae aliquam taxam solventibus reservatur. Quare usus *pew rent* in America, quo soluta pecunia quis obtinet locum in scamno, huic canoni non adversatur." *Epitome Iuris Canonici*, II, n. 585.

however, seems to be based on a misconception. The pews in the American churches are fixed seats, not comparable to the movable chairs commonly used in France and Italy. When a person, therefore, rents a pew, he does not rent a seat which may be moved to any part of the church, but one that is located in a certain specified place which he has chosen or which has been assigned to him by the pastor. The place, therefore, rather than the pew, is rented. If pew 1, which A has rented, is, for any reason whatever, moved to some other location in the church, and pew 2, which is rented to B, is placed where pew 1 formerly stood, according to the ordinary understanding of the system of pew-rent, A can reasonably expect that this pew 2 will be reserved for him rather than for B, who had occupied it in its former location. It is because of this fact that the place rather than the pew is considered in renting a pew, that a larger rent is customarily asked for the better situated seats.

Cocchi [18] seems to hold the same opinion as Vermeersch-Creusen, but the German authors, who are better acquainted with the pew-rent system, practically without exception, hold that it does apply.[19]

If Canon 1263 is then taken to apply to the system of renting pews, its regulations will be found to be very practical. The ordinary is to decide whether pews are to be rented or not, and his express permission is required if the practice is to be introduced. But since the renting of pews is an immemorial custom in this country, extending back, as it does, at least to the year 1842, it may be continued without the ordinary's express consent as long as he tolerates it. Since the promulgation of the Code, many ordinaries have, however, in their synodal decrees, expressly mentioned it as an approved mode of revenue.[20]

---

[18] *Commentarium in Cod. I. C.*, III, n. 96, b.

[19] Grünewald, *Die Rechtesverhältnisse an Kirchenstühlen*, p. 59; Hilling, *Das Sachenrecht des Cod. I. C.*, p. 157; Eichmann, *Lehrbuch des Kirchenrechts*, §168, p. 408; De Meester, *Compendium*, III, n. 1255; Prümmer, *Manuale I. C.*, p. 469.

[20] Cf. above, note 16.

The ordinary is instructed not to permit individuals to rent pews if this should discommode the rest of the faithful too much. The source of this legislation is to be found in a decision of the Congregation of Rites,[21] which, adverting to the fact that some persons reserved a number of pews for themselves, and thereby forced others to stand, advised bishops to correct this abuse. There is not much danger of such disregard of the rights of others creeping into the system of pew-rent as it exists in this country. The reservation is generally restricted to certain functions, outside of which anybody may occupy the seat. Another restriction is often added, according to which the reservation ceases as soon as the services have begun. Should the renter, therefore, come late, e.g., for the principal Mass on Sunday, when the reservation holds, he has no right to expect that another person who has taken his place should leave it. Should he come to another Mass, even though early enough, he could not claim his place either.

The Canon also states [22] that, in all such reservations of a definite place to an individual, the tacit condition is included permitting the ordinary to revoke them at any time, for a just cause, i.e., if the common welfare is thereby furthered. He can, therefore, order that the renting of pews be abolished and all seats declared free, in the interests of the poorer members of the parish, or to prevent the development of class distinctions or factions within the parish, or to put an end to disturbances during the services arising from this cause. In fact, he is empowered to dispose of it in any way he sees prudent or necessary, whenever the private rights come into conflict with the public interests.[23] He can do this, no matter how long the practice has existed, or without taking into consideration the length of time that any individual has held, or has acquired the right to hold such a seat. In the last case, equity might require that the individual be repaid the rent for the future reservation, of which he has been deprived. Beyond this, however, the holder can claim nothing.

---

21 S. R. C., Dec. 11, 1604—*Decr. Auth.*, n. 174.

22 Can. 1263, §3.

23 Grünewald, *Die Rechtsverhältnisse an Kirchenstühlen*, p. 58-59.

The purpose of this legislation is to enable the ordinary to crush any abuses that may arise, or that may already exist, in connection with the pew-rent system. Experience shows that abuses can arise very easily.[24] The undeniable fact that this system is liable to sharpen class lines in the parish, is the most serious objection that can be brought against it. Instead of all the faithful being equal in the House of God, the preferable seats are reserved for the richer members, since they are able to offer higher rents. The Fathers of the Third Plenary Council of Baltimore recognized this danger in particular and tried to guard against it.

> In unaquaque ecclesia constituatur spatium liberum ubi fideles Sacro adesse et verbum Dei audire possint. In hoc autem spatio eligendo et in eorum usum aptando, nunquam obliviscatur ille, qui ecclesiae praeest, hos homines esse Christi pauperes, et Boni Pastoris exemplo misericorditer cum illis agat, seduloque vitet quidquid eos contemnendi aut pudefaciendi specimen prae se ferre possit. Secus enim (quod Apostolus expresse vetat), exhonorantur pauperes (Jac. II, 2–6), et timeri aliquando potest ne per pastorem ecclesiae ii, pro quorum aeque ac pro divitum animabus rationem est redditurus, a divino cultu et a vita Christiana penitus arceantur.[25]

Because of this and other objections, as also because of the development of better and more equitable methods of support, the custom of renting pews is gradually dying out.[26]

One of the results of the introduction of the pew-rent system in this country was the formation of a custom, according to which persons became members of the parish in which they had rented a pew. This custom was recognized and tolerated, either tacitly or expressly, by the ordi-

---

[24] Cf. Grünewald, *op. cit.*, pp. 5, 11, 12 and 13.

[25] Conc. Plen. Balt. III, n. 289.

[26] Jansen, "Church Support," *Hom. and Past. Rev.*, XXVIII (1927), 266; Sans Souci, "Weekly Envelope Collection," *Am. Eccl. Rev.*, LXII (1920), 577; Grünewald, *op. cit.*, p. 13.

naries. The Fourth Diocesan Synod of Louisville, held in 1874, decreed:

> Subditi autem cujusque pastoris censentur illi tantum qui, vel intra congregationis suae limites a Nobis statutos, ut statuendos, degunt, vel in ecclesia scamna vel sedem (a pew or seat), conducunt, *etiamsi extra limites pastori assignatos, domicilium habeant.*[27]

In the Second Diocesan Synod of Philadelphia, Bishop Kenrick also mentioned this custom and said that it could be tolerated, although he wished to have each one join the parish within whose limits he lived.

> Ut omnia ordine procedant,...certos assignabimus limites, pro temporum et adjunctorum varietate, intra quos pastores diversarum ecclesiarum et Missionarii munera sua exerceant;...*Habita ratione consuetudinis iam invalescentis,* quam tamen cupimus emendatam, *permittimus ut iis qui scamna in ecclesia aliqua conducunt, vel eam noscuntur constanter frequentare, omnia sacramenta ab ejusdem ecclesiae pastore, si requisitus fuerit, administrentur, licet extra limites designatos morentur.*[28]

May this custom still be observed after the promulgation of the new codification? That it is contrary to the common law, which states that domicile is to determine parish membership,[29] is evident. It has been stated[30] that this custom could not be an immemorable custom against the common law, because the United States did not come under the rule of the common law until 1909. Before that date the United States were under the jurisdiction of the Sacred Congregation for the Propagation of the Faith; and, as far as its effect on the Church in the United States was concerned, there was no common law. Accordingly, it is maintained, this custom, contrary to the common law, could only date from the year 1909, and must, therefore, be abolished.

---

27 Synodi Dioecesanae Ludovicopolitanae IV, V, VI (1896), cap. X, n. III, p. 15.

28 Constitutiones Dioecesanae (1842), p. 14, n. 5.

29 Can. 94, §1.

30 "Determination of Membership in a Parish," *Am. Eccl. Rev.*, LXXXII (1930), 423, gives an exposition of this view.

One fact is certain. The custom existed, as a custom, before 1909, and still exists[31] as a custom, which now is contrary to the common law. Now, does Canon 5 mean that only those contrary, existing customs may be tolerated which have been immemorably (if the word may be used) contrary to the common law, or does it also include other customs, which now are contrary, but which formerly were not? If the former is the right interpretation, then the Church would seem to be favoring those who rebelled against her former legislation, by legalizing their rebellion. At the same time she would be punishing those who, possibly for uncounted generations, have fostered a custom which was in accord with her former law, by demanding that they abolish it immediately, because it now is contrary to her law. This would hardly seem to be her intention. Nor do the words of the Canon require this interpretation. It merely says that customs existing at the present time, which are contrary to the Code, without any distinction as to whether they were formerly contrary or not, may be tolerated under certain circumstances.[32]

Another question: Are only those customs, no matter whether they were *contra, praeter*, or *secundum ius*, included in Canon 5, which had some actual connection with the common law; or are those also included which were formed under another law of the Church, e.g., this custom of pew-rent determining parish membership in the United States under the jurisdiction of the Propagation; or even such customs which had no connection with any Church law whatever, e.g., one formed in countries to which no knowledge of the Church's existence had ever penetrated? *Ubi lex non distinguit, nec nos distinguere debemus.* Canon 5 says nothing whatever about the necessity of this custom having been formed under the influence of the common law. It merely says, customs actually existing, which now are contrary to the common law. Therefore, there does not

[31] Cf. Synodus Dioec. Syracusensis Undecima (1922), n. 64.

[32] Cf. Augustine, *Commentary*, I, 76; also Woywod, *Commentary*, I, 3.

seem to be any reason to reject the custom in question, because it was not formed under the egis of the common law.

Another objection may, however, be raised against the validity of this custom. Before 1918, there was no custom of joining a parish by paying pew-rent, because there were no parishes to join. Before the Code, the common law required that, for the erection of a canonical parish, there be some certain source of income, other than voluntary contributions. Since, practically speaking, voluntary contributions were the only source of revenues in the churches of the United States, no canonical parishes could be established. There may have been a few parishes which had some other stable source of income, but these few exceptions would not militate against the force of the argument that, since there were no canonical parishes to join, there could not be any custom sanctioning a certain, peculiar method of joining such parishes.

However, here again the same stubborn fact shows itself. There was a custom of joining ecclesiastical congregations in that way. The essential element of that custom seems to have consisted in this, that by renting a pew the renter was recognized as a member of that congregation, irrespective of whether it was merely a so-called "mission," a parish in the broad sense of the word,[33] or a strict canonical parish. If any strict canonical parishes did exist in the dioceses of Louisville and Philadelphia, there was no prohibition against joining these parishes in this manner. Whether, by renting a pew, they joined a mission or a canonical parish, would, therefore, seem to have been considered altogether secondary, compared to the essential point that they were permitted to join them in this way. Consequently the opinion, which holds that the custom continued through the changes of 1909 and 1918, if the ordinary tolerated it, seems probable. Some ordinaries refused to tolerate it, explicitly declaring that domicile shall decide

---

[33] The word "pastor" is employed in the quotations from the decrees of Louisville and Philadelphia, given above.

membership in a parish.[34] Other ordinaries, however, still recognize and tolerate the custom.[35]

The conclusion to be reached, therefore, seems to be that the custom, according to which a person became a member of a parish by renting a pew, is an immemorial custom, contrary to the common law, and it is left to the judgment of the ordinary, whether it can be prudently abolished or not. That its abolition, if this can be done without too serious disturbances, is advisable, is evident, since it will prevent abuses and enable the pastor to know accurately who belongs to his flock.

Sometimes people wish to rent a pew in another than their own parish, not because they thereby wish to join this parish, but for some other reason, e.g., because they frequently attend services in this second parish. This practice is altogether legitimate, as long as they fulfill their obligations in their own proper parish, and no particular statutes forbid it. The statutes of the diocese of Crookston prescribe: "As a general rule pews should be rented only to the parishioners. No pastor is allowed to rent pews to a person or family belonging to another parish unless he has made certain that the person or family have a pew in their own proper parish." [36] Other ordinaries have made similar regulations.[37]

B.—Assessments

Another popular system of quasi-compulsory Church support in this country is the assessment plan, according to which every adult member of the parish, or every family,

---

[34] Synodal Decrees of the Diocese of St. Cloud, n. 77: "Catholics not belonging to a national church must adhere to the parish in which they live."

[35] Syn. Dioec. Syracusensis Undecima (1921), n. 64: ". . . Porro tamen, habita ratione consuetudinis, indulgemus ut iis qui in ecclesia aliqua absque fraude legis scamna conducta jam antea, scil., unam mensem, habebant, Sacramenta omnia administrari possint ab hujus ecclesiae parocho, etiamsi alibi domicilium habeant. (Syn. Syr. I, 69)." Cf. "Pew Rent and Domicile," *Am. Eccl. Rev.*, LXXIV (1926), 413, on this subject.

[36] Statutes of the Diocese of Crookston, n. 25.

[37] Syn. Dioec. Buff. Vigesima Septima, Art. 496; Syn. Dioec. Harrisburgensis Octava, n. 366.

agrees to contribute a certain amount for the support of religion. Gasquet mentions that such voluntary assessments were occasionally resorted to in the Middle Ages to meet extraordinary expenses for which the tithes or the voluntary collections of the faithful were not sufficient.[38] In the early days of the American Church, Catholics on the frontiers frequently employed this plan, sometimes in novel ways, to ensure the establishment and support of a church in their community. Thus, in the latter part of the eighteenth century, the Catholics in Kentucky agreed to set aside the hundredth bushel of grain for the support of the missionary who ministered to them.[39] The difficulty of gathering such a tribute from the widely scattered members of the flock does not seem to have occurred to them. It may, however, help explain the fact that hardly a tenth of even this small assessment was actually paid.[40] Such conditions were, however, abnormal, and did not militate against the inherent soundness of the system itself. Many synods have, therefore, recommended this plan as a laudable method of raising revenues.[41]

The assessment idea is carried into practice in a variety of ways, all of which may be divided into two general groups. The methods of the first group are all based on the idea of having the faithful agree to contribute a certain specified amount, irrespective of their own financial status. Thus, each family or each adult member of the parish is expected to contribute his annual "Dues," as this payment is known in Irish communities, or "Kommunikantengeld," in German parishes. The size of this payment is determined by the needs of the parish. This system has been very widely used, especially in small communities with a comparatively stationary population, where the difference between the rich and the poor is not too marked. The

[38] Gasquet, *Parish Life in Medieval England*, p. 124.

[39] Webb, *Centenary of Catholicity in Kentucky*, p. 166.

[40] *Ibidem.*

[41] Among the later synods: Sixth Dioc. Syn. of Boston (1919), n. 175; First Syn. of Altoona (1923), n. 132; Twenty-seventh Dioc. Syn. of Buffalo (1924), n. 490; First Dioc. Syn. of Crookston (1921), n. 404; Eighth Dioc. Syn. of Harrisburg (1928), n. 360.

"Dollar-a-Sunday Plan," a recent development of this idea, is proving very popular.[42]

The second group, being more closely based on the idea underlying the tithing system, has proven even more popular. The ratio of the needs of the parish with the income of its members is determined, and every member is then asked to pledge that proportion of his income. It is evident that, in determining the proportion, due allowance must be made for those who, either because of negligence or of inability, will not contribute their share. These payments may be made annually or in installments, to suit the convenience of the parishioners. Monthly or weekly envelopes for the payment of these installments are frequently introduced.

Various methods are also used to determine the amount which each one is to contribute. A certain percentage may be specified, and the actual contributing of that percentage then left to the conscience of the individual. Or the pastor, with the help possibly of a special committee chosen by himself or elected by the parish, will determine how much each person is expected to give. Parishioners may be asked to sign a pledge stating how much they will give. These, or other similar devices, are in use wherever the assessment plan is used.

The reason for the widespread use and popularity of these methods of proportional assessment is to be found in their intrinsic soundness and justice. If such a system is introduced and carried into practice with even a fair degree of thoroughness and accuracy, most of the parishioners will contribute their just proportion, or at least an amount approaching it, to the support of religion. The ordinary Catholic realizes that it is his duty to contribute his share, and is willing to do so without the need of too much urging. But, if he should suspect that he is being imposed upon, that he is expected to give considerably more than his proportion to compensate for the refusal or negligence of others, it is but human that he himself will also moderate his generosity. The employment of some such method of

---

[42] Cf. *The America*, XLI (1929), 234.

support, which is based on a proportional assessment, frees him from these suspicions and induces him to give willingly.

The definite specification of how much is expected of them also has the advantage of giving peace of conscience to sincere Catholics. The main purpose of the science of Moral Theology is to determine, as accurately as possible, the import and the extent of the various obligations which God has placed upon men. In the training of her clergy the Church insists that they be well grounded in this science, for upon them rests the duty of instructing the faithful as to what their obligations are and what they must do to fulfill them. Now, it hardly seems consonant with their office as pastors of souls, for the clergy to continually impress upon the faithful the gravity of the obligation of supporting the Church without at the same time informing them how much they must contribute to fulfill this obligation. To say that their consciences must be their guides is begging the question. Conscience itself needs a guide, and it is the purpose of Moral Theology to furnish this guide, and the duty of the clergy to give it to the people. By determining definitely the extent of this obligation of Church support, the clergy are, therefore, merely fulfilling their duty, and thereby saving their charges from scruples of conscience in regard to the extent of this obligation of supporting religion.

The proportionate assessment plan has another decided advantage. Records are generally kept indicating how much each one has contributed. The periodic publication of the list of contributors, and the amounts contributed, will serve as a prod to urge on those Catholics who are inclined to be careless or negligent, to a better observance of this obligation. Although the Church is averse to the employment of force in raising revenues, the use of moral suasion, or of the power of human respect, as an added incentive for doing that which is good, can hardly be condemned.

Some, indeed, deprecate the publication of the names of donors and amounts donated, saying that this induces the faithful to contribute, not because of a supernatural motive, but because of the honor and respect which they expect to obtain. That this may be true to some extent cannot be denied. Nevertheless, the good results of this practice would seem to outweigh the evil.

The generous contributors are thereby held up as a good example for the others. Although Christ told His followers that they should not seek to advertise their good deeds, that their left hand should not even know what their right has done,[43] He also counseled them to give a good example to others: "So let your light shine before men that they may see your good works and glorify your Father Who is in Heaven." [44] The knowledge that others are doing their full duty will be a great encouragement to those who are generous, and a rebuke to the negligent.

The Church has always recognized the power of human motives to induce the faithful to do good. During the first centuries the Deacon, at a certain part of the Holy Sacrifice, publicly announced the names of all those who had contributed at the Offertory.[45] Although, according to the testimony of St. Jerome,[46] this policy occasionally led to various abuses, she did not abandon it. When the list of contributors became too long, at least the names of those who had specially distinguished themselves for their generosity were still mentioned.[47] In 666, the Council of Merida decreed:

> Presbyter in singulis quibusque Ecclesiis, quibus iussus fuerit per sui Episcopi ordinationem praeesse, pro singulis diebus Dominicis Sacrificium Deo procuret offerre; et eorum nomina, a quibus eas Ecclesias constat esse constructas, vel qui aliquid his sanctis Ecclesiis videntur aut visi sunt contulisse, si videntes in corpore sunt, ante altare recitentur tempore Missae, quod si ab hac decesserunt aut discesserint luce, nomina

[43] *Mt.*, VI, 3.

[44] *Mt.*, V, 16.

[45] Link, *Mess-Stipendien*, p. 28.

[46] *In Ezechielem*, c. 18—*MPL*, XXV, 175: "Multos conspicimus, qui opprimunt per potentiam vel furta committunt, ut in suis sceleribus glorientur, publiceque diaconus in Ecclesia recitet offerentium nomina; tantum offert ille, tantum ille pollicitus est, placentque sibi ad plausum populi, torquente eos conscientia."

[47] Link, *Mess-Stipendien*, p. 30.

eorum cum defunctis fidelibus recitentur suo in ordine.[48]

The special privileges and honors given to the patrons of churches, the prominent display and perpetuation of the names of donors of various objects connected with the church building, such as altars and windows, all these show that the Church is willing to employ human means and human motives to encourage others to greater generosity. The publication of the names of the contributors in a parish is, therefore, not opposed to, but in conformity with the general policy of the Church.

Because of all these and other reasons, the generality of the faithful are heartily in favor of the proportionate assessment plan. The clergy are even more enthusiastic in their praises, wherever the system has been introduced. They also are relieved by the certainty that they are not asking the more sincere and willing parishioners to make undue sacrifices, to give more than their just share. Being assured of a dependable, sufficient income, they no longer see themselves compelled to insist, in season and out of season, on the obligation of supporting religion. This one advantage of the proportional assessment system, that it frees the pastor from the necessity of continually speaking about financial matters, is in itself sufficient to counterbalance any possible evils that might be connected with this plan.[49]

C.—Seat-Money.

As a substitute for pew-rent, the custom of collecting seat-money has been introduced in various places. This practice has received official recognition and approval in the statutes of a number of dioceses.[50] This method of obtaining funds appears to have been suggested by the custom found in some of the European countries of paying a

---

[48] C. 19—*Mansi*, XI, 86.

[49] Prosit, "Income Assessment for Church Uses," *Am. Eccl. Rev.*, LXII (1920), 468.

[50] Among others: Sixth Dioc. Syn. of Boston (1919), n. 175; Seventh Dioc. Syn. of St. Louis (1929), n. 162; Eleventh Dioc. Syn. of Syracuse (1922), n. 71.

small fee for the use of a chair in the church. Among the principal factors which have led to its introduction and spread are the following. The continual shifting of the population in the cities, due to the fact that ever greater numbers of people live in rented quarters, results in a constant and large change of personnel in the members of the different parishes. Most of these new parishioners do not expect to remain long in the place, and, therefore, neglect to rent pews or become otherwise affiliated with the parish. When the income from the renting of pews decreased, the pastor found himself compelled to find other means of revenue to replace that which he lost. In many cases he turned to the seat-money system for relief.

Even if all the parishioners of the average city parish would be willing to rent pews, the pastor would be unable to accommodate them. The number of seats in most city churches is out of all proportion to the number of members, as is evident from the fact that as many as six to eight Masses are required on Sundays to accommodate all the parishioners. Justice demanded that the burden of Church support should be distributed over all the parishioners rather than that it be limited to the comparatively small number to whom pews could be rented. In some places pews were rented repeatedly, according to the number of services on Sunday. In most places, however, the collecting of seat-money was introduced.

This collection may be taken up in any one of a number of different ways. In some places the ushers ask for the contribution at the entry to the pew, when they show the people to their seats. In others it is taken up during the Mass, each worshipper being approached individually, or a collection, distinct from the Offertory collection, being taken up. Envelopes are sometimes used in connection with this system.

The seat-money collection has a number of advantages to favor its introduction. In the ordinary city parish the receipts from this system are much larger than those which would be obtained from pew-rent. It also frees the pastor from the necessity of keeping the accurate records which are required for the satisfactory operation of the pew-rent system. It prevents any abuses which might arise from the more or less permanent reservation of certain pews for certain individuals. It distributes the burden of support over the entire body of worshippers.

But it also has its serious disadvantages. No distinction is made between the rich and the poor, both classes being expected to contribute like amounts. If an attempt is made to free the poor from this payment, by setting aside a certain block of seats for their use, such an advertisement of their poverty cannot help but be an humiliation for them. The holding of a special collection, or the taking up of the seat-money, as the people enter the pews, will tend to give undue prominence to financial matters. However, some of these evils are unavoidable, under the present circumstances, if the parish is to be supported.

D.—Door-Collections

Although the practice of collecting at the doors of churches has been discouraged from its very origin, and has been repeatedly condemned, it has, nevertheless, become a widely used method of quasi-compulsory Church support in the United States. This collection seems to have originated around the middle of the last century, in three lake cities of the Cleveland diocese.[51]

This innovation was quickly brought to the attention of the Holy See, for in 1859 Cardinal Alexander Barnabo, the Prefect of the Sacred Congregation of the Propaganda Fide, adverted to it.[52] In 1861, the fathers of the Third Provincial Council of Cincinnati took it under consideration. After considerable deliberation[53] the conclusion was reached[54] that the difficulties which were urged against this custom did not exist, i.e., that it did not prevent people from attending services and from receiving the Sacraments or hearing the Word of God. It was, therefore, decided

---

[51] Conc. Prov. Cincinn. III (1861), Tertia Cong. Priv.—*Coll. Lac.*, III, 220-221.

[52] In a letter of Feb. 19th, 1859, mentioned in the Third Private Congregation of Conc. Prov. Cincinn. III—*Coll. Lac.*, III, 220.

[53] Cf. *Coll. Lac.*, III, 219-221.

[54] Tertia Cong. Priv.—*Coll. Lac.*, III, 220-221.

to leave it to the prudence of the ordinary of the Cleveland diocese, whether this practice was to be tolerated in the localities where it already existed or whether it should be abolished. Its introduction in other places was, however, to be prevented.[55]

In ratifying the decrees of this council, Pope Pius IX declared, however, that the decision reached in the third private congregation, regarding the door-collection, did not meet his approval. He therefore asked that the bishop of Cleveland be instructed by the Sacred Congregation of the Propaganda Fide to eliminate this practice within two years.[56] Whether this was done or not is unknown to the author. The practice itself, however, spread to other dioceses, and is now found in operation in many sections of the country.

As a general rule, the door-collection is restricted in its use to city parishes which have a constantly changing membership, or where large numbers of transients come for services. According to circumstances, more or less compulsion is employed in taking up this collection. In some places the ushers merely stand near the doors and call the attention of those who enter the church to this collection by displaying some coins in their hands. Nothing may even be said to those who enter without making the customary offering. In other places money changing tables and signs indicating the amount that each one is expected to give are placed in the vestibule of the church. Sometimes tickets are even given in exchange for the contribution, which are then gathered up by the ushers as they show the people to their seats. According to the system used and the character and temper of the pastor and his corps of ushers, the door-collection may, therefore, be anything. It may be merely a courteous reminder of the duty of Church support, availing itself of the power of human respect as a sanction to give it effectiveness; or it may be a scandalous imitation of the entrance fee exacted at places of public amusement.

---

[55] *Ibidem.*

[56] Letter of Card. Alexander Barnabo, Prefect of the Cong., to Archbishop Purcell of Cincinnati, VI Kal. Feb., 1862—*Coll. Lac.*, III, 229-230.

As a justification, those who have introduced the door-collection claim that it is the only possible means at their disposal for the raising of sufficient funds to enable the parish to exist. Pew-rent and assessment systems have been tried and proven failures because the one element most necessary for their success, a parochial membership, the major portion of which is stable, is lacking in these parishes. The few stable parishioners, forming only a small group in the total number of worshippers, were either unwilling or unable to support the necessary establishment, and the voluntary contributions of the transients to the Offertory collection were too insignificant to better the situation. Unless some way could be found to make all the worshippers help to support the parish, it would have to close its church and school, and also discontinue all other activities. The only practical way to get the necessary support was to ask for the contributions of all at the door, as they entered the church. In short, the door-collection was indispensable.

Many apologists for this system of Church support freely admit that abuses may arise in connection with this collection, that even such serious scandal may sometimes result as to induce some of the faithful to give up their religion. The door-collection, they admit, can never be an entirely satisfactory method of raising funds, no matter how carefully abuses are guarded against, and how mildly the collection may be enforced. It always will appear to strangers who do not understand it, as a fee which must be paid to attend the Holy Sacrifice. It makes no distinction between the rich and the poor. And if the poor are permitted to pass without making any contribution, the publicity of this mock charity will be an intolerable shame to those who have to receive it.

Nevertheless, although they see and deplore all the dangers and disadvantages inherent in the door-collection, those who defend its use sincerely believe that it is the lesser of two evils. Desperate needs justify the employment of desperate remedies, as long as they are not evil in themselves. It is better, they maintain, to take these risks, to suffer the occasional defection from the Church, than to paralyze the various activities of the Church or to deprive the entire community of the services of religion, results which would almost inevitably follow the abolition of this collection.

All of these arguments are of no avail, however, since they are answered by the definite decision of the Church. In her disciplinary regulations she has repeatedly and explicitly reprobated the door-collection, and ordered that it be entirely abolished.

Although, as was mentioned above, the Holy See attempted to eradicate this practice in its very infancy, it continued, nevertheless, and spread to other dioceses. In correcting the Acts and Decrees of the Second Plenary Council of Baltimore, held in 1866, the Sacred Congregation of the Propaganda Fide asked that the following amendment be introduced:[57] "Praxim, si qua existat, pecuniam exigendi ad fores ecclesiarum, ut fideles ingredi possint, et divinis mysteriis adesse, sibi minime placere declaravit Summus Pontifex Pius Papa Nonus, et eliminandam prorsus voluit." The fathers of the Council, therefore, expressed it as their desire that an end be put to this custom of demanding a fixed sum of money, in the form of a fee, from the people who came to attend the Holy Sacrifice and to hear the Word of God.[58]

The Third Plenary Council of Baltimore renewed the condemnation of the previous Council,[59] and called attention to the fact that this condemnation was based on the direct instructions of the Holy Father. Nevertheless the practice continued, and still exists.

Having received and investigated a number of complaints, Archbishop Falconio, Apostolic Delegate to the United States, felt compelled to send a circular letter to

---

[57] Instructio S. C. de Prop. Fide Generalis, de Decretis Conciliis corrigendis, n. 18—*Coll. Lac.*, III, 381.

[58] C. Plen. Balt. II, n. 397—*Coll. Lac.*, III, 506.

[59] C. Plen. Balt. III (1884), n. 288. "Praxis, sicubi forte existat, pecuniam exigendi ad fores ecclesiae Dominicis ac Festis diebus, ut quis ingredi possit ac sacrosancto missae sacrificio interesse, jampridem eliminari debuisset. Eam enim damnavit Summus Pontifex Pius IX et prorsus tollendam significavit. Decessores quoque nostri supremo ejus judicio obsequentes finem pravae huic consuetudini omnino imponendum esse statuerunt."

the American ordinaries, on September 29th, 1911, in which any practice whatever of collecting at the door, even under the plea that it was a seat-collection was distinctly forbidden.[60] In the legislation of the Code, the prohibition of the door-collection has been extended to the Universal Church, and all contrary customs are reprobated.

Canon 1181.—**Ingressus in ecclesiam ad sacros ritus sit omnino gratuitus, reprobata qualibet contraria consuetudine.**

Similar decrees, forbidding collections at the doors of churches, have been included in the statutes of a number of dioceses.[61]

In view of all these clear and unequivocal prohibitions, only one course remains open; to submit one's personal and fallible judgment to the decisions of the Church; to labor for the abolition of this system of Church support, and depend upon Divine Providence and the native ingenuity of the American clergy to replace it with a more acceptable and less dangerous source of revenue. Various methods will suggest themselves as worthy of trial. The collecting of seat-money, although it also has its disadvantages, and may lend itself to abuses, is, however, considered as less likely to lead to abuses, and might be employed as a substitute. The envelope system might be used to advantage in connection with the seat-money collection. Ushers could distribute envelopes, either when they show the people to their seats, or at any suitable time before the collection is taken up. Upon these envelopes a suggestion could be

[60] *Am. Eccl. Rev.*, XLV (1911), 594: "I, therefore, request you to command all rectors of churches in your diocese to discontinue all these practices, if they have already been introduced, and by no means to permit them to be established, if they do not already exist. I well know that in some churches money is collected at the door, not for mere entrance, but as a payment for a seat in the church. Even this practice cannot be tolerated, since it produces an undesirable impression on all, and has proved to be, in practice, the cause of many regrettable consequences."

[61] Sixth Dioc. Syn. Decrees of Boston (1919), n. 187; Los Angeles Diocesan Statutes (1927), n. 220; Statutes of the Twenty-seventh Dioc. Syn. of Buffalo (1924), n. 491; Statutes of the Diocese of Crookston (1921), n. 348; Statutes of the Diocese of Oklahoma (1913), n. 186.

printed, indicating how much is asked, and directing that the envelopes be returned with the contribution in the Offertory collection.

By such and other means which would suggest themselves the immediate gap left in the parish finances by the abolition of the door-collection might be filled. As for the future, whether such methods would have to be permanently retained, or whether a more stable method of support may gradually evolve with the changing circumstances and conditions, would remain to be seen. And even if, here and there, it would be found to be necessary to close a church building, and possibly suppress a parish or unite it to another, because of lack of support, this would not necessarily be an unmixed misfortune. The members of such parishes could easily be apportioned to the neighboring parishes, which the event might act as a shock to make the faithful realize that the Church cannot continue her work of salvation, unless they, by their united efforts, contribute the necessary means.

3.—Methods of Voluntary Support

A.—Donations and Legacies

Donations and legacies, as sources of revenue for the Church, have already been treated above when speaking of the ways and means by which endowments can be formed. Under the subject of donations, however, there remains the question of the small donation, which is generally known as an alms. Canon 1503 regulates this method of support.

Canon 1503.—Salvis praescriptis can. 621–624, vetantur privati tam clerici quam laici sine Sedis Apostolicae aut proprii Ordinarii et Ordinarii loci licentia, in scriptis data, stipem cogere pro quolibet pio aut ecclesiastico instituto vel fine.

The practice of begging alms from house to house, for pious purposes, has always been a prolific source of abuses, in spite of the Church's attempts to guard against them.[62]

[62] Doheny, *Church Property, Modes of Acquisition*, p. 50, note 3.

In the United States, the Third Council of Baltimore tried to regulate the begging of alms. Complaints had frequently been voiced, both by the clergy and the laity, regarding the numbers and the importunity of the priests who came from other regions to gather these alms. The Council pointed out that they often neglected to obtain the permission of the ordinary or of the rector of the parish, that they even continued to solicit sometimes in spite of a direct prohibition, thereby giving scandal and causing serious inconvenience to the local religious activities and institutions. To put an end to these abuses, it was decreed [63] that the rectors of parishes should not permit anybody, who was known to be collecting alms, to celebrate the Holy Sacrifice in their church, even a single time, until this person had obtained the permission of the local ordinary to collect alms. This was the only possible remedy at the disposal of the rector of the parish, since he could not prevent anybody from actually going around among the parishioners and asking them for money. The local ordinary was also instructed not to grant this permission unless he had previously been asked in writing by the mendicant's proper superior to give his permission. If these conditions were not fulfilled, the offending solicitor was to be reported to his proper superior, and if even this should prove ineffective, to the Sacred Congregation of the Propaganda Fide.

These conditions, under which alms may be lawfully collected, are preserved in Canon 1503. No private person, be he laic or a cleric, is to gather alms for religious purposes until he has obtained the permission of the Holy See or of his proper ordinary, and also of the ordinary of the place where he intends to solicit. Religious mendicants are governed by special rules laid down in Canons 621–624, and in the decree of the Sacred Congregation of Religious, November 21st, 1908.[64] This Canon does not prohibit pastors from collecting alms within their own parishes, since they act in their official capacity when doing this.[65] To collect

---

[63] Conc. Plen. Balt. III, n. 295.

[64] *AAS*, I, 153.

[65] Canon 415, §2, 5° for secular pastors, and Canon 630, §4, for religious. Cf. Vermeersch-Creusen, *Epitome*, II, n. 823.

outside of their own territory, however, the proper permissions must be obtained.

Because of many and serious abuses, the Holy See has repeatedly found it necessary to publish special regulations regarding the collecting of alms by Orientals in Latin countries.[66] The latest pronouncement on this matter is a decree of the Sacred Congregation for the Oriental Church, January 7th, 1930.[67] The main provisions of this decree are:

1. The permission of the Sacred Congregation for the Oriental Church must always be obtained before any Oriental cleric, no matter what his rank or dignity be, can collect any money, be this in the form of alms or Mass Stipends, in any Latin diocese.

2. As a general rule this permission will not be given.

3. If, for very extraordinary reasons, the permission is granted, it will only be given for certain definitely specified territories, whose local ordinaries will be individually and expressly notified of the fact and of the reasons for granting the permission. Even then the consent of the local ordinary must be obtained by him who has obtained this permission from the Holy See.

4. Unless he has received such a notification from the Holy See, either directly or through its Delegates, no ordinary is allowed to grant his permission to an Oriental to collect, nor can he or the rector of any church give such an Oriental any Mass Stipends. Should they, nevertheless, do this, they themselves will be held accountable for the celebration of these Masses, or for any money whatsoever which has been received or collected by an Oriental.

5. These rules apply to all Orientals everywhere, except those who are in their own Oriental territory. (No doubt Oriental pastors, legitimately appointed in Latin dioceses and under Latin ordinaries, are also excepted, and may col-

---

[66] S. Cong. de Prop. Fide, 12 Apr., 1894—*Coll.*, n. 1866; S. Cong. pro Ecclesia Orientali, Aprilis, 1928—*AAS*, XX (1928), 107, et Maii, 1928—*AAS*, XX (1928), 161.

[67] Decretum III—De Clericis Orientalibus Eleemosynas, Pecuniam vel Missarum Stipendia Colligentibus seu Corrogantibus extra Orientales Regiones, et Dioeceses.—*AAS*, XXII (1930), 108.

lect alms from their own Oriental parishioners, without having to obtain permission from anybody; and from the Latin faithful in their own diocese if they obtain their ordinaries' permission. This exception seems to be indicated by the title of this decree, "...outside of Oriental regions, and [of their] dioceses.")

6. Ordinaries are requested to acquaint their clergy, and if necessary, the faithful, with the provisions of this decree.

B.—The Offertory Collection

The collection taken up during the Holy Sacrifice of the Mass, generally known as the Offertory Collection, holds the distinction of being one of the oldest methods of Church support. Together with the tithes and the first-fruits, it can trace its origin back, through the Apostolic times, to the Old Law. When God prescribed for His chosen people, during their wanderings in the desert, what sacrifices were to be offered up to Him, He also specified which of these sacrifices, or what parts of them, were to fall to the lot of the priests as their portion.[68]

After the Sacrifice of the New Law had been instituted, the bread and the wine which was used for the Sacrifice was generally offered by those who were present and partook of the Sacrifice. Everyone who came brought his contribution. This custom seems to have been so universally accepted that if anyone neglected to make his offering it became a source of wonderment, possibly even of scandal[69] for the other faithful. St. Cyprian, talking about almsgiving,[70] takes the occasion to rebuke a certain person for not bringing the customary offering when coming to the Sacrifice: "Thou art rich and wealthy, and presume to celebrate the Eucharistic Sacrifice without having contributed to the offering, since you have come to this Sacrifice without any offering, but rather partake of the Sacrifice which the poor have provided."

---

[68] Cf. *Lev.*, I-VII.

[69] Thurston, "Stipends for Masses," *The Month*, CXI (1908), 17.

[70] *De Oper. et Eleem.*, cap. XV—*MPL*, IV, 612. St. Cyprian died in the year 258.

After the reading of the Scriptures and the preliminary prayers which formed the Mass of the Catechumens, when the time came for the actual Sacrifice the Celebrant remained at the altar chanting, together with the singers, one or more psalms, while the Deacon and Subdeacon gathered up the offerings and brought them to the altar to be blessed by the Celebrant. These offerings usually were far in excess of what was needed for the actual Sacrifice.[71] That which was to be used for the Sacrifice was then separated, the remaining portions being kept on or near the altar until after the Mass. A part of this was then distributed as *eulogiae,* blessed bread, to be consumed by those present.[72] The greater portion, however, which was still left over, was then distributed among the clergy for their support, and for distribution to the poor.[73] A description of this practice is found in the Apostolical Constitutions:[74]

> Those eulogies which remain over after the celebration of the mystical offerings, let the deacons distribute them among the clergy, according to the direction of the bishop or presbyter; to a bishop four parts, to a presbyter three parts, to a deacon two parts, and to the rest of the subdeacons or readers or singers or deaconesses, one part.

In the Canons of Theophilus[75] this division among the clerics of the offerings that remained after the celebration of the mysteries is also prescribed.

Already by the beginning of the third century these offerings had gradually become more varied, until regulations had to be laid down as to what species of contributions could be offered at the altar. Oblations of grain, grapes, oil, and incense, since they were intended for use in the Sacrifice, might be made at the altar and at the Offertory collection, even though they were not actually used for that purpose. All other contributions, such as first-fruits of all

---

[71] Thurston, "Stipends for Masses," *The Month,* CXI (1908), 17.

[72] Danzer, "Der Klingelbeutel," *LQS,* LXXXI (1928), 160-161.

[73] Shields, "Mass Honoraria," *Irish Eccl. Rev.* Ser. 5, Vol. XXXI (1928), 130; cf. also Thurston, *op. cit.,* p. 18.

[74] Lib. VIII, 31—*MPG,* I, 1127.

[75] Can. 7—*MPG,* LXV, 42. Theophilus was an archbishop of Alexandria, and died in 412.

other produce and of animals, were to be offered either before the Mass, or at least before the reading of the Gospel, or else they were to be taken directly to the dwellings of the bishop and the clergy.[76] But if they were offered before or during the first part of the Mass, these offerings were not to be brought up to the altar, since they were not so intimately connected with the Sacrifice.[77] And if any bishop or presbyter, "contrary to the law of God as instituted by Him concerning this Sacrifice," should bring any other offering than those permitted to the altar, as, for instance, honey, milk, vinegar, or any flesh or plants, the Apostolic Canons decreed that he should be deposed.[78] The III Council of Carthage, held in 397, also decreed: "That in the Sacrament of our Lord's Body and Blood nothing further should be offered than that which our Lord Himself handed down, namely, bread and wine mixed with water; nor shall there be offered anything else except grapes and wheat and corn." [79]

The faithful realized, however, the tremendous efficacy of this Sacrifice, and wished to share more fully in the graces flowing from it, by bringing their oblations into as intimate connection with it as they could. They, therefore, persisted in their efforts to bring their oblations to the altar itself, upon which this Sacrifice was consummated. The Abbot Regino who, in his enumeration of the details which the bishop had to watch over,[80] doubtless was guided by the existing laudable or tolerated customs, advises that if any of the faithful should insist on making their offerings at the altar itself, of such gifts as were not included among those to be made at the Mass, but were, nevertheless, intended for the use of the altar, as, for instance, candles,

---

[76] Shields, *op. cit.*, pp. 131 and 133.

[77] *Canones Apostolorum*, can. IV—*MPG*, CXXXVII, 42.

[78] Can. III—*MPG*, CXXXVII, 38-39. Although this work, *Canones ecclesiastici Sanctorum Apostolorum*, is apocryphal, and originated during the third century, according to Maroto, *Institutiones I. C.*, I, 51, it serves to indicate what the practice was at the time and place of composition.

[79] Can. 23—*Mansi*, III, 922.

[80] *De Eccl. Disc. et Relig. Christ. Inquisitio*, lib., II, n. 72—*MPL*, CXXXII, 190. Regino, a Benedictine Abbot of Prum, died in 915.

they are to offer them before the Mass, or before the reading of the Gospel. All these regulations and restrictions show that the early Christians looked upon this right to bring their contributions to the altar as a great privilege, through which they participated in the special fruits of the Mass, the *fructus ministerialis*.[81] A special commemoration was originally also made after the Secret of the Mass, for all those who had contributed.[82]

This practice of contributing at the Mass varied considerably in different places and at different times, according to the local customs which were developed.[83] In itself, however, it was so continuously and widely observed, that it came to be regarded as an obligation. When the decline of the practice of daily Communion which had served to foster this Offertory contribution, and the gradual lessening of the first fervor led to a neglect of this custom, its preservation was attempted by the stressing of the obligatory force. The Council of Macon, which had set as its goal the counteracting of the prevalent laxity in regard to religious duties, ordained:[84] "Furthermore, we decree that on all Sundays an offering of bread and wine be made to the altar by all the faithful, men and women." All those who resisted this decree were to be anathema.[85] A king of the Franks, who like most of the civil rulers of that time, felt himself called upon to regulate the affairs of both the Church and the State, ordained that the faithful were to make daily offerings to the priests if this were possible; and if it should not be possible to make them daily, they must without any default at least make them on Sundays.[86] Regino, in his *Inquisitio*,[87] advises:

> That on visitations the bishop is to inquire if both men and women make an offering of bread and wine, and if the men do not then he is to inquire if the

[81] Danzer, "Der Klingelbeutel," *LQS*, LXXXI (1928), 162.
[82] *Ibidem.*
[83] Shields, *op. cit.*, p. 131; Thurston, *op. cit.*, p. 17.
[84] C. Matiscon. (585), can. 4—*Mansi*, IX, 951.
[85] *Ibidem.*
[86] Capit. Karoli Mag. et Lud. Pii, VI, can. CLXX—*Mansi*, XVIIb, 951.
[87] Lib. V, n. 89—*MPL*, CXXXII, 287.

women (their wives) make an offering for them and for all the household, as is contained in the Canon.

These and similar regulations at least helped to preserve this praiseworthy custom from being completely neglected or forgotten. But it was no longer as strictly observed as in the earlier ages of the Church; not everyone who was present brought his contribution. In the course of time it had lost its obligatory force and had become an entirely voluntary collection. Burchard of Worms, who lived around the beginning of the eleventh century, describes it as follows:[88]

> The offertory having been said, if there are such as wish to make an offering, the celebrant goes to the epistle side, and standing there with uncovered head and with his left side turned to the altar, he takes his maniple from his left arm, and holding it in his right hand he offers the upper part of it to be kissed by each individual who makes an offering, saying: May your sacrifice be acceptable to the Omnipotent God; or, May you be repaid a hundredfold and may you possess eternal life.

From the fact that a description of the Mass, written in the sixteenth century, advises the celebrant to say a psalm or some other prayer while the collection is being taken up, so that he may then offer up these contributions with the paten, Danzer [89] concludes that, at that time, the number of those making an offering must generally have been small, since the time occupied in saying one psalm was sufficient to take up this collection.

Long before this the Offertory collection had undergone another change. Instead of bread and wine and other articles of food, money was now being offered in various localities. Honorius of Auton, writing about the year 1020, mentions that this change has already taken place, "for, as the faithful do not communicate, the large offerings of bread and wine proved superfluous, and it was decreed that the former offering in kind be replaced by a money offering,

---

88 *Ordinarium Missae,* cf. Danzer, "Der Klingelbeutel," *LQS,* LXXXI (1928), 161.

89 "Der Klingelbeutel," *LQS,* LXXXI (1928), 161.

so that instead of offering loaves, the faithful should offer money, which, in turn, shall be given to the poor or shall be expended on the uses pertaining to the Holy Sacrifice." [90] Just when this change occurred cannot be definitely determined. But by the beginning of the thirteenth century, offerings in kind were abolished everywhere.[91]

During the following centuries the Offertory collection custom was no longer so rigidly and universally observed, as the needs of the Church, in different places, were amply provided for from other sources, such as the tithes and the endowments. But it was never entirely abandoned. Gasquet, in his description of the Church in England shortly before the Reformation, mentions that this collection was taken up with more or less regularity in most places, according to the needs of the parish.[92] How intimately in the estimation of the people this collection was connected with the services, is illustrated by the fact that, when large numbers of the faithful fell away from the Church and established the Protestant religions, one of the customs which they retained was that of taking up a collection during the services. The plate collection of the present-day Protestant churches, therefore, is a survival of the traditional Offertory collection of the Catholic Church.

During colonial times the Church in the United States was almost entirely supported from the proceeds of the property belonging to the Jesuit Fathers in Maryland.[93] As soon as the Church began to spread these proved insufficient. The Synod of Baltimore thereupon ordered the introduction of the Offertory collection to help raise the necessary means.[94] "Statuimus igitur ut in singulis congregationibus duo aut tres praecipuae virtutis ac auctoritatis viri, tanquam Ecclesiae curatores a Pastore, vel ab ipsis

---

[90] *Gemma Animae*, lib. I, cap. LXVI—*MPL*, CLXXII, 564.

[91] Shields, "Mass Honoraria," *Irish Eccl. Rev.*, Ser. 5, Vol. XXXI (1928), 137; cf. also Thurston, "Stipends for Masses," *The Month*, CXI (1908), 20.

[92] *Parish Life in Medieval England*, pp. 129-130.

[93] Shea, *History of the Catholic Church in the U. S.*, I, 451, and II, 260.

[94] Acta et statuta Synodi Dioecesanae Baltimorensis (1791), n. 6—*Coll. Lac.*, III, 3; cf. also n. 5 and 23, of the same synod.

congregationibus eligantur, atque ut Dominicis et festis diebus curatores taliter constituti, post lectum in Missa Evangelium, collectionem oblationum faciant." Since then the Offertory collection has been a permanent institution in the Catholic Church of the United States.

In various places of this country it is customary for the Offertory collection to be taken up by clerics, sometimes even by the celebrant. For the celebrant to leave the altar during the Mass to pass around the collection plate certainly seems to be opposed to the spirit of the Church's liturgical rules. In the rubrics for the celebration of the Holy Sacrifice[95] the Church prescribes that, after the celebrant has begun the Mass, by making the sign of the Cross at the foot of the altar, he is not to pay any attention to anyone who may be saying Mass at another altar, not even if the latter should be at the Consecration. He is to continue his Mass without interruption to the end. In view of this strict instruction, she can hardly tolerate that the celebrant should interrupt his Mass and leave the altar, even the sanctuary, to take up a collection. Therefore, even if it should not cause scandal or excite ridicule, this custom, so radically opposed to the liturgical rules of the Church, would have to be condemned. The Second Plenary Council of Baltimore reprobated this custom in no uncertain terms.[96]

> Fertur vero, quod non sine maximo animi dolore accepimus, nonnullos aliquibus in locis esse Sacerdotes, qui ipsa intra Missarum solemnia, ab altari recedant, aedemque sacram circumeant, a singulis fidelibus eleemosynam petentes. Quem turpissimum abusum, Ecclesiae sacrisque ejus ritibus injurium, quique Catholicorum ruborem et indignationem, Acatholicorum vero irrisionem et contemptum provocat, reprobamus et prorsus exstirpandum decernimus. Qua in re singulorum Episcoporum conscientia oneratur.

Not only the celebrant, but the ministers also were forbidden to take up this collection. The Third Council of

---

95 *Missale Romanum*, Ritus Servandus in Celebratione Missae, III, 4.
96 Conc. Plen. Balt. II, n. 364—*Coll. Lac.*, III, 496.

Baltimore, adverting to this condemnation expressed by the Second, renewed it *verbatim.*[97]

Is it permissible for other clerics than those engaged at the altar to take up this collection? There does not seem to be any regulation forbidding it. Its introduction in places where the faithful are not accustomed to it could hardly be recommended, as it would be likely to cause considerable misunderstanding and even scandal. Whether the faithful in this country, no matter how long the custom has existed, ever become reconciled to it is hard to judge. Many of them, as also many clerics, take exception to it as unbecoming to the priest.

Danzer, however, points out[98] that in the first centuries of the Church the ministers of the Mass, especially the Deacon, were supposed to take up this collection. The cleric, in his opinion, represents the Deacon who gathered the offerings of the faithful, and brought them up to the altar. He claims that this practice impresses more deeply upon the people the close relation between this collection and the Holy Sacrifice itself. The cleric should, therefore, wear an ecclesiastical garb when performing this action. He mentions, apparently with approval, that up to the present time this collection is still taken up in Poland by a priest wearing a surplice and stole.

That the ministers of the Mass took up the collection in the early ages cannot be denied. It is also true that this tended to impress upon those present the intimate relation between the Holy Sacrifice and the gifts of the faithful offered during the Sacrifice. There is, however, one important difference between the Offertory collection of the first centuries and the same collection in later ages. The Deacon in the early Church gathered the offerings of the people, which consisted of bread and wine, part of which was used immediately in the Holy Sacrifice itself. Would the early Church have prescribed that the Deacon should take up this collection, if the people had, as they do at the present time, offered money which was to be used to pay the butcher, the baker, and the candlestick maker? The fact, as was

---

[97] Conc. Plen. Balt. III, n. 293.

[98] "Der Klingelbeutel," *LQS*, LXXXI (1928), 162.

mentioned above, that the faithful were instructed to bring such offerings as were not intended for direct use on the altar, not at the Offertory, but before the Mass or before the Gospel, or preferably even directly to the dwellings of the clergy, might give an indication of the intention of the Church.

But since there is no direct prohibition, custom will have to decide whether or not this collection is to be taken up by clerics. The introduction of this practice in places where it does not yet exist, does not seem advisable however, as it is too liable to shock and scandalize worshippers. For the celebrant, or the other ministers of the Mass, to take up the collection would be to act in direct contradiction to the statutes of the Church in this country, as decreed in the Second and Third Plenary Councils of Baltimore, whose decrees on this subject are still in force.

4.—Extraordinary Methods of Support

It often happens that a parish or an ecclesiastical institution finds its regular income insufficient for its ordinary expenses, or for some special expense, such as building or extensive repairs. In such circumstances recourse is often had to some extraordinary means to raise the required revenue. This extraordinary source of income may be intended for temporary or permanent use, depending on whether it is meant to provide for a temporary or continual need. Some of these methods are so generally used that they might be called an ordinary means of support, except for the fact that the revenues from them, with few exceptions, are merely considered as an incidental addition to the regular income.

The most common source of supplementary income is the votive stand. The faithful make an offering for a candle or a votive light before a statue or picture of our Lord or of one of the Saints. The little sacrifice, the idea of the sacrifice being also carried out in the burning of the candle, is intended to increase the devotion of the suppliant, and, at the same time, render the prayer more effective by the addition of the sacrifice. This beautiful and centuries-old

Catholic custom, which expresses so aptly the vitality and the sacrificial spirit of Mother Church, while at the same time it tends to give the church or chapel a more pleasing and devotional aspect, deserves to be retained.

Abuses, however, have to be guarded against in this custom. Catholics have been accused of superstition in connection with this practice, of believing that the offering of a candle was an infallible means of obtaining that which they desired. Some of the simpler people may have believed this, just as some may still believe it. A little instruction on the significance and efficacy of this practice, when the occasion offers, might, therefore, prove beneficial.

A greater danger, however, is to be seen in the tendency, which occasionally shows itself, of commercializing this devotion, and thereby causing the Church to be ridiculed. A good illustration of this tendency is found in a news article which appeared in a secular daily during the past year. Although a little long, it may be worth while to reproduce it. It is as follows:

> An "illuminable votive device" invented by the Rev. ——, will be used for the first time at 10 o'clock Sunday morning, when the new St. Anthony shrine will be inaugurated. The Rev. —— has applied for a patent on the device.
>
> The device is operated by electricity and takes the place of the old-fashioned votive lights using oil or some other substance. It is operated by a coin-receiving arrangement. Two rows of large candles in the rear of the bank will be lighted when a dollar is inserted in the slot. The two front rows will be operated by 50-cent pieces, the smaller lights by 25-cent pieces, and the smallest of all by dimes.
>
> "Christians at all times have made use of votive lamps to demonstrate their reverence and devotion toward sacred persons and objects," said the Rev. Mr. ——. "All over the world, whether it is the noblest of cathedrals or the humblest of chapels, the custom of burning a votive light in honor of God and His saints is in evidence.

> "The votive light ordinarily is made up of a small receptacle filled with olive oil, but more generally of a hard substance, made from mineral oils and animal substances. This last has proved objectionable for many reasons. To allay these objections the more modern and more suitable mode of illumination will be employed in the new St. Anthony shrine. A simple operation and the devotee sees his votive light burning brilliantly before his favored shrine." (Sic!)

The remarks of the cleric who sent this specimen may serve as an indication of the reaction of the overwhelming majority of Catholics to such methods.

> Enclosed clipping is offered without comment. But I ask you,...is there nothing that could be done about such a shameless bid for shekels? Why must we stand about and allow it to be presumed that we are all seeking to fill our coffers by means of "hard substances made from mineral oils and animal substances," and ready to pay the Rev. Mr. —— royalties on his "illuminable votive device?" While he is moved by the spirit of invention might he not plan a baptism device, and a prayer device, and even a Mass device, to shorten the labors and to enhance the revenues of the clergy? And, in all seriousness, is not the "illuminable votive device" the *reductio ad absurdum*, the perfect and irrefutable condemnation of all votive stands? Or is it?

The house-to-house collection is another method of obtaining additional funds for some special purpose, such as the erection of new buildings, improvements, or extensive repairs. The pastor and his assistants make an effort to see each family and ask them for as substantial a donation as they can afford. This is generally a gruelling task, but the results will also be proportionately satisfactory. It is an alms collection, but with this difference, that a larger donation is asked for, and the appeal is based not only on charity, but also on justice, the duty of the parishioners to support their parish. In some places this collection is combined with the taking of the census and has become an annual affair.

Another form of this same collection is the block collection. Each family is approached once a week or once a month, and asked for a small donation which they have agreed to give. This collection may, however, be included under the assessments system as a regular means of support, because of the specified amount given and the stability of the income which it provides. All of these collections are instituted by the pastor in his official capacity for the support of the parish. No permission need, therefore, be obtained from anyone.[99] These visits also tend to strengthen the spiritual bond between the pastor and his flock, and will enable him to labor more effectively for their spiritual welfare.

Picnics, excursions, and fairs are also conducted occasionally to help raise funds. Similar festivals were already held in the Middle Ages for the same purpose.[100] Some of the traditional sports and customs, which were observed at these medieval celebrations, were of such a nature that the Church authorities found it prudent to prohibit them.[101] The Second Plenary Council of Baltimore pointed out [102] that at the present time also these picnics, etc., frequently were the direct occasion of scandal and sin. It, therefore, called upon ordinaries to permit them only under proper precautions, or, if they deemed it necessary, to prohibit them altogether. The Third Plenary Council of Baltimore added certain restrictions.[103] It forbade their continuation into the night, or the use of any spirituous liquors, and prohibited them altogether on Sundays and certain other days. These and similar regulations have also been incorporated into the particular statutes of many dioceses.[104]

The holding of dances for the promotion of pious works was absolutely forbidden by the Third Plenary Council of

---

[99] Cf. Canons 415, §2, 5° and 630, §4.

[100] Gasquet, *Parish Life in Medieval England*, p. 241.

[101] *Ibidem.*

[102] Conc. Plen. Balt. II, n. 396—*Coll. Lac.*, III, 506.

[103] Conc. Plen. Balt. III, n. 290.

[104] Among others: Diocesan Statutes of Harrisburg (1928), n. 365; Boston Synodal Decrees (1919), n. 188; Los Angeles Diocesan Statutes (1927), n. 225; Statutes of the Diocese of Buffalo (1924), Art. 494, 1.

Baltimore.[105] In 1916 a decree of the Sacred Congregation of the Consistory [106] strengthened this regulation of the Baltimore Council and urged its stricter observance.

All clergymen, secular as well as regular, are strictly forbidden to promote or favor dances or balls, even if these should be held to help and support a good and pious cause or for any other purpose; besides all clergy are prohibited to attend such dances if arranged by laymen.[107]

To settle doubts, a later decree [108] declared that all dances, even though they be held during the day or in connection with picnics, were included in this general prohibition.

Appeals for help sent through the mails are a fruitful source of income. This method is chiefly employed by charitable and educational institutions, especially such as are more or less engaged in missionary work. The use of the mails has been discovered to be a more satisfactory and less costly means of obtaining the needed funds than the sending out of persons to solicit alms. The fact that these appeals are frequently so numerous and insistent as to become somewhat of a nuisance does not militate against the use of this means. It does, however, indicate the multiplicity of these worthy enterprises and, if one is to judge from the results, the surprising generosity of the faithful, when they are convinced of the merit of the appeal and the genuineness of the need.

Is this method of collecting alms included under the prohibition of Canon 1503? Augustine [109] maintains that, since the Canon "does not distinguish between personal or oral quests and begging by letter," it is included. The opposite opinion, however, seems to be more probable because of both the intrinsic and extrinsic [110] reasons in its favor.

---

105 Conc. Plen. Balt. III, n. 290.

106 S. C. Consist., Decretum *Circa Quasdam Choreas*, die 31 Martii, 1916—*AAS*, VIII (1916), 147.

107 *Ibidem.*

108 S. C. Consist., Declaratio *Super Decreto De Choreis*, die 10 Dec., 1917—*AAS*, X (1918), 17.

109 *The Pastor according to the New Code of Canon Law*, p. 211.

110 Vermeersch-Creusen, *Epitome, I. C.*, II, n. 823. Cocchi, Vromant and De Meester are mentioned in this place, as also holding this opinion.

The danger of abuses and scandal, which caused the prohibition of the collecting of alms by private persons, unless the required permissions are first obtained, is far less when there is question of begging through the mails. Besides, as Vermeersch-Creusen point out,[111] it would be almost morally impossible to obtain the permission of all the ordinaries, into whose territories these letters are to be sent. Another argument is drawn from the prescriptions of the decree *Singulari quidem,* which regulated the collecting of alms by religious women. This decree expressly permits the Superioresses of religious institutes to send begging letters, unless the legitimate superior for some just cause has forbidden it.[112]

Abuses, however, are not entirely excluded from this practice. Some of the appeals for help are so crudely worded, or the promised expressions of gratitude, such as Masses and prayers offered up for benefactors, are enumerated so explicitly and in such detail as to leave an impression of bargaining the spiritual for the temporal, in other words, of simony. It is, indeed, lawful and proper that these needy institutions should make the only return in their power to their benefactors, their prayers. But good sense and tact will have to be used, lest the receivers of these letters be offended and scandalized by an appearance of commercialism in the whole transaction.[113] Chain-letters, if any are received, should be entirely disregarded.

Besides these, there are many other methods which may be used to swell the income of the Church. Some of these are card parties, dinners, lotteries, silver teas, the formation of clubs or societies to provide for certain needs, the pub-

---

[111] *Loc. cit.*

[112] S. C. EE. et RR., 27 Martii, 1896—*ASS*, XXVIII (1895-96), 555-558: IV: "Nihil tamen impedit, quominus Superiorissae, nulla petita licentia, ad sublevandam Domuum vel piorum operum, quibus praesunt inopiam, possint eleemosynas . . . etiam per litteras impetrare ab honestis ac benevolis personis quibuscumque, usquedum a legitimo Superiore, rationabili ex cause, non prohibeantur."

[113] Cf. "With Scrip and Staff," *The America*, XLI (1929), 233-234.

lication of, or the taking up of subscriptions for magazines, the selling of devotional objects, etc. Before employing any of these methods the prudent pastor will consider any possible evils that may be connected with them. All of them, if used with discretion and without too much profusion, will help, not only financially, but also spiritually, by drawing Catholics closer together and developing the spirit of service and sacrifice for the Church.

CHAPTER FOUR

Support of Diocesan and Extra-Diocesan Activities

One of the problems to which the American system of Church financing has given rise is that of obtaining a sufficiently large diocesan income to provide for the proper maintenance of the local ordinary and of the diocesan curia. The provisions of the common law, relating to this question, have been evolved from the conditions that existed in countries where the Church has been long established. They have been, and still are, entirely inadequate to provide for the exigencies of the Church in this country. A brief review of the diocesan sources of income, as provided for in the common law, will lead to a better understanding of the entire subject.

The first Christian congregations were generally established in cities and towns. At the head of each congregation or church, the equivalent of what is now known as a diocese, was the bishop. All the Church revenues and properties were entirely under his control. He administered them, either directly or indirectly through his deacons, without having to give an account to anybody except God. The revenues he disposed of as needed for his own support, for the support of the other clergy, and for the relief of the poor.[1] Other churches, which were later erected within the episcopal city, were dependent on the bishop's church, the cathedral. All of them formed one parish. Their properties and revenues were not kept separate, but were massed with the temporalities of the cathedral into one whole, under the administration of the bishop.[2]

---

[1] Pöschl, *Bischofsgut und Mensa Episcopalis*, I, 10; Ratzinger, *Geschichte der kirchlichen Armenpflege*, pp. 73 and 122.

[2] Boudinhon, "Mensa, Mensal Revenue," *Cath. Ency.*, X, 194; Thomassinus, III, 2, 1.

The revenues were originally divided into four parts, one portion for the bishop's use, another for the rest of the clergy, a third for almsgiving to the poor, and the remaining fourth for the upkeep of the church buildings and for the expenses connected with the public worship.[3] A different division was sometimes introduced, but these same needs were always provided for.[4]

As the Church grew and congregations were established in the surrounding country by the clergy whom the bishop sent out to convert the people, this strictly centralized administration became too unwieldy. Before long these country parishes administered their own properties, and spent their revenues for the needs of their own church and the support of the clergy attached to it.[5] In the course of time many of the filial churches also became independent parishes, and acquired the same separate administration of their revenues and properties.[6] All these parishes remained, however, under the jurisdiction of the bishop and formed his diocese.

Owing to various circumstances the temporalities of the cathedral were also divided. These enormous endowments, which formed the Church-states of the Middle Ages, often came under the control of ambitious and worldly prelates who squandered the revenues in the furthering of their own purposes. The needs of religion were then neglected, so that the clergy occasionally found themselves in actual want. This led to the separation of a portion of this endowment, the revenues from which were intended for the

---

[3] Ratzinger, *op. cit.*, p. 120; Thomassinus, III, 2, 13, n. 1-2.

[4] Cf. c. 23-30, C. XII, q. 2, and c. 1-3, C. X, q. 3, regarding the threefold or fourfold divisions, which were most commonly in use.

[5] Pöschl says that it has been generally held that originally the properties of these churches were also administered directly by the bishop, that everything was given to him, and he gave back whatever amount he considered expedient or necessary, just as he did in regard to the cathedral and its filial churches in the episcopal town. He denies that these outlying parishes ever were under this central administration, and attempts to prove that, as soon as these country congregations were established, they retained and administered their own properties, separate from that of the cathedral. *Bischofsgut und Mensa Episcopalis*, I, 14-32.

[6] Ratzinger, *op. cit.*, p. 203.

support of divine services and of the cathedral clergy and diocesan officials. Later another portion was set aside for the personal needs of the bishop. These endowments formed the *Mensa Capitularis* and the *Mensa Episcopalis,* and their revenues provided for the diocesan needs.[7] There was, therefore, no necessity of imposing a tax upon the parishes for the support of the ordinary and of the diocesan officials. Many of these endowments were lost during and following the Protestant Reformation. In almost all cases, however, arrangements were made by which the State agreed to provide for the maintenance of those for whom this endowment was intended.[8]

The *Cathedraticum,* as a means of revenue, is entirely distinct from the *Mensa Episcopalis.* As parishes were established the rectors of these parishes also acquired the management of the income. But as a token of reverence and subjection to the bishop, each of these churches, independent in regard to their temporalities, paid a tribute to the mother church, the cathedral, hence the name *Cathedraticum.*

In the earlier ages this payment was made rather through custom than through law.[9] The first mention of this *cathedraticum* is found in the decrees of the Council of Braga, which was held in 572.[10]

> Placuit ut nullus episcoporum, per suas dioeceses ambulans, praeter honorem cathedrae suae, id est duos solidos, alius aliquid per ecclesias tollat, neque tertiam partem ex quacumque oblatione populi in ecclesiis parochialibus sibi usurpet; sed ecclesiae reparationi servetur, et singulis annis episcopo ratio fiat.

After this various laws were promulgated by Popes and Councils regulating the payment and the amount of this tribute.[11] It always remained a nominal tax, usually two

---

[7] Pöschl, *op. cit.*, II, 63 et seq., and I, 5.

[8] One of the most recent examples of State support is found in the renewal of the Concordat between the Holy See and Prussia, Art. 4—*AAS*, XXI (1929), 525.

[9] Fanning, "Cathedraticum," *Cath. Ency.*, III, 441.

[10] C. 1, C. X, q. 3.

[11] "The Cathedraticum," *The Pastor,* V (1886), 323-325; Doheny, *Church Property, Modes of Acquisition,* p. 54.

solidi, or their equivalent.[12] Its principal purpose was not so much to furnish the means for the support of the ordinary, but rather to serve as a mark of reverence and subjection. This still remains the motive.

Canon 1504.—Omnes ecclesiae vel beneficia iurisdictioni Episcopi subiecta, itemque laicorum confraternitates, debent quotannis in signum subiectionis solvere Episcopo cathedraticum seu moderatam taxam determinandam ad normam can. 1507, §1, nisi iam antiqua consuetudine fuerit determinata.

This Canon does not determine the amount, but states that it shall be moderate, and is to be determined in the provincial councils or in a meeting of the bishops, if it has not yet been determined by ancient custom. That it is still intended to be a tribute of respect, rather than a means of support has again been stressed in a recent decision.[13]

Besides the *cathedraticum,* the Third Lateran Council also permitted ordinaries, for manifest and reasonable causes, to ask in all charity for a moderate assistance, in case of some special necessity.[14] This *subsidium caritativum,* as it is called, is also permitted by Canon 1505 of the Code.

Canon 1505.—Loci Ordinarius, praeter tributum pro Seminario, de quo in can. 1355, 1356, aut beneficialem pensionem de qua in can. 1429, potest, speciali dioecesis necessitate impellente, omnibus beneficiariis, sive saecularibus sive religiosis, extraordinariam et moderatam exactionem imponere.

Canon 1506 also permits the ordinary to impose a regular tribute, for the good of the diocese, upon churches, benefices and other ecclesiastical institutions, but only on the occasion of their foundation or consecration. This he could

---

[12] According to Augustine, *The Rights and Duties of Ordinaries,* p. 385, two solidi were equivalent to about six dollars.

[13] S. C. C., Dioecesis N. et aliarum in Gallia, 13 Martii, 1920—*AAS,* XII, 446.

[14] C. 6, X, *de censibus, etc.,* III, 39; Cappello, *De Visitatione,* I, cap. III, tit. 18.

also do under the former discipline.[15] After these benefices, churches or other institutions have been founded or consecrated he can no longer impose such a tax, nor increase one that has been imposed.

Canon 1506.—Aliud tributum in bonum dioecesis vel pro patrono imponere ecclesiis, beneficiis aliisque institutis ecclesiasticis, quanquam sibi subiectis, Ordinarius potest tantummodo in actu fundationis vel consecrationis; sed nullum imponi tributum potest super eleemosynis Missarum sive manualium sive fundatarum.

Where it is customary the ordinary may also receive the procurations to defray the expenses of the diocesan visitation. The chancery may also collect a small fee for certain dispensations.

Canon 346.—. . . circa vero victualia sibi suisque ministranda vel procurationes et expensas itineris, servetur legitima locorum consuetudo.

Canon 1056.—Excepta modica aliqua praestatione ex titulo expensarum cancellariae in dispensationibus pro non pauperibus, locorum Ordinarii eorumve officiales, reprobata quavis contraria consuetudine, nequeunt, occasione concessae dispensationis, emolumentum ullum exigere, nisi haec facultas a Sancta Sede expresse eis data fuerit; et si exegerint, tenentur ad restitutionem.

According to the common law, therefore, both before and after the promulgation of the new codification in 1918, the diocesan needs were to be provided for by the revenues from the following sources:

1. Income from the *Mensa Episcopalis,* the diocesan endowment, which is expected to furnish the bulk of the necessary revenues.

2. The *Cathedraticum,* a small tax to be paid each year by every church and benefice subject to the bishop.

---

[15] Ayrinhac, *Administrative Legislation in the New Code of Canon Law,* p. 399.

3. For occasional and special needs the *subsidium caritativum* may be levied upon all beneficiaries, but only upon their beneficial revenues.

4. Tributes imposed at the time of foundation or consecration of benefices, other ecclesiastical institutions and churches.

5. The procurations, to provide for the expenses of the diocesan visitation, if custom permits.

6. Certain small chancery fees.

Beyond these the ordinary is to impose no further taxes upon his subjects.[16] This same prohibition existed before 1918. Thus the Third Lateran Council had decreed:[17]

> Prohibemus insuper, ne ab abbatibus, vel episcopis vel aliis praelatis novi census imponantur ecclesiis, nec veteres augeantur, nec partem redituum suis usibus appropriare praesumant; sed libertatem, quam sibi maiores conservare desiderant, minoribus quoque suis bona voluntate conservent. Si quis vero aliter fecerit, irritum quod egerit habeatur.

What is the effect of this legislation on the question of diocesan support in the United States? With a few possible exceptions, there are no endowments for diocesan purposes. That which the Church intended to be the main source of revenues for diocesan expenses is, therefore, ruled out at the very beginning. If the *cathedraticum* is to be a nominal payment, equal to about six dollars, according to Augustine,[18] it will be of little more practical value than the revenues from the non-existent endowments. The *subsidium caritativum* is not intended to be a source of regular income, and must also be left out of consideration. When benefices, which are almost always parochial, are founded, or churches consecrated, these parishes ordinarily are themselves in serious financial straits. The imposition of a special tribute, which the older and richer parishes are not required to pay, upon these new and struggling parishes, would certainly not be equitable. The other two sources,

---

[16] Canon 1506.
[17] C. 7, X, *de censibus, etc.*, III, 39.
[18] *The Rights and Duties of Ordinaries*, p. 385.

the procurations and chancery fees, will also be of little moment. The ordinary then has practically no income. This state of affairs has existed in the United States since the Church was established in this country. Some method of obtaining sufficient revenues necessarily had to be found.

After prescribing that the Offertory collection was to be taken up for the support of the Church, Bishop Carroll, in the diocesan synod of Baltimore, decreed how the proceeds were to be used.[19] According to the ancient usage, the offerings were to be divided into three parts, one for the support of the priest, another for the poor, and the third for the needs of divine service. No mention was made of a fourth portion for the bishop. This was not necessary at that time, as Bishop Carroll had other means of support, viz., a portion of the revenues of the former Jesuit estates in Maryland and Pennsylvania.[20]

Other prelates were not so fortunate. When Fenwick went to Cincinnati in 1822 as its first bishop, his entire resources consisted of the Sunday collections in his chapel, which ranged from one to three dollars each Sunday. From this he had to support himself and two priests. He went to Europe to solicit help, and was able to obtain about $10,000.[21] Other bishops obtained the means for their support from some special provisions made in their favor,[22] or by acting as the pastors of the cathedral or of some other large parishes.[23] They also received occasional donations from other parishes at the time of the diocesan visitation.

Such an unsatisfactory arrangement could not long continue. Attempts were, therefore, made by various ordinaries to provide themselves with sufficient revenues on a more equitable basis. The Acts of the First Diocesan

---

[19] Acta et Statuta Synodi Dioec. Balt. (1791), n. 7—*Coll. Lac.*, III, 3.

[20] Shea, *The History of the Catholic Church in the U. S.*, III, 66.

[21] Shea, *op. cit.*, III, 345-346.

[22] Thus Archbishop Marechal of Baltimore received $1000 annually from the "Corporation of the Roman Catholic clergymen," which had been formed by the disbanded Jesuits in the country to hold and administer the property which their Society had owned. Cf. Shea, *op. cit.*, III, 70.

[23] For an example, cf. Shea, *op. cit.*, III, 547-549.

Synod of New York contain a long dissertation on this matter.[24] Bishop Hughes states that it has been customary in that diocese for the bishop to draw a pension from the cathedral as its pastor. This income, however, was not sufficient. For further support the ordinary had to depend on the uncertain gifts of the parishes, when he made the annual visitation. These donations were large or small, or even entirely refused, dependent on whether or not the trustees of these parishes were satisfied with the bishop's conduct. When they did give him a donation, it was done in such a way as to leave the impression that it was an entirely gratuitous offering, a mere act of charity. The right of the ordinary, as the first pastor of the diocese, to be supported by his flock, was entirely ignored. He, therefore, called upon the clergy to see to it that all the parishes helped to provide him with a decent and honorable income. The details of how much each parish was to contribute he left the clergy to decide.

Earlier in the same year Bishop Kenrick of Philadelphia had voiced the same complaints at the diocesan synod.[25] The clergy recognized the justice of his remarks and agreed that all the parishes should contribute for diocesan purposes. Nine rectors of parishes, in different sections of the diocese, were selected and were told to determine how much each parish should give. When they made their report, the entire body of the clergy approved it and promised that their parishes would pay the amounts which they had been assessed.

In both of these cases there was no mention that these payments were regarded as a *cathedraticum*. They were voluntary assessments, imposed upon all the parishes according to their size and financial ability. The purpose in both cases was to provide the ordinary with a sufficient income for his needs, on the principle that the bishop, even more than the rest of the clergy, had the natural right to be maintained by the contributions of the faithful.

---

[24] Decreta Syn. Dioec. Neo-Ebor. Primae (1842), n. 29.

[25] Acta Synodi Secundae Phil. (1842), p. 11.

The method employed was indeed not sanctioned by the common law; the conditions, however, being as they were, some extra-canonical means had to be used.

When the First Plenary Council of Baltimore was celebrated in 1852, no official action was taken in regard to this problem. That it was discussed by the assembled bishops can be deduced from the letter of Cardinal Fransoni, Prefect of the Sacred Congregation de Propaganda Fide, to the Archbishop of Baltimore.[26]

> Relatum est in Plenaria Synodo pertractatum quoque fuisse de ratione aliqua ineunda ut ad onera sui muneris sustinenda Episcopi juvari possint subsidiis ex propriis dioecesibus. Aequum profecto id videtur. Quum tamen multiplex proponi methodus valeat, Antistitum sententia erit exquirenda: per Metropolitanos vera facile Amplitudo tua praestare id poterit. Supervacaneum tamen haud erit innuere Praesules Canadenses superiore anno ea de re pertractasse, cum proposuerint ut vel liceret accipere tertiam partem proventuum unius paroeciae, aut duarum paroeciarum in dioecesi; vel quartam aut quintam partem, si inter tres aut quatuor paroecias divideretur onus; vel decimam partem reddituum, si inter plures, aut fere omnes paroecias supradictum onus divideretur, habita ratione circumstantiarum. S. Congregatio propositionem ultimo loco exhibitam censuit potius esse amplectendam, atque ad eum scopum, SSmo Domino Nostro probante, in favorem Canadensium Antistitum fuit latum decretum.

In the First Provincial Council of Quebec, the Canadian prelates had decided to petition the Holy See for faculties in perpetuity permitting them to tax their parishes for diocesan purposes, in one of the ways mentioned in the above letter.[27] The Sacred Congregation de Propaganda Fide granted them the permission to tax their parishes up to one-tenth of their income. This arrangement, however,

---

[26] Letter of Oct. 23d, 1852—*Coll. Lac.*, III, 153.

[27] Cf. Letter of the Rt. Rev. Prince, Mar. 15, 1852—*Coll. Lac.*, III, 621.

was contrary to the common law, and was to continue only until the Holy See would make other provisions.[28]

No definite method was, however, agreed upon for the support of the bishops in the United States. In a later letter [29] the Sacred Congregation of the Propaganda Fide approved a suggestion, which had apparently been made, that, for the present, a declaration of the ordinary's right to demand an income adequate for his needs should be sufficient. Further proposals were to be expected from the provincial councils.

A few years later the first Provincial Council of Cincinnati offered the following suggestion:[30]

> Morem gerentes monito S. C. de Prop. Fide opportunum esse duxerunt Patres, supplicari Sanctae Sedi, ut dignetur rationem uniformem sancire, qua Episcopi hujus Provinciae ad onera muneris sui sustinenda subsidiis ex Ecclesiis propriae jurisdictionis juventur.

The Holy See, however, refused to prescribe any one method for use in all the dioceses of the province, no doubt, because it realized that the conditions in one diocese might be altogether different from those in another, even if both were in the same province. It pointed out that it had already acknowledged the right of the ordinary to demand that his subjects contribute for his support. But the application of this principle, the determination of how much they were to contribute and the method in which this should be done, could be best effected in the diocesan synods.[31] The reply seems to indicate that this solution had already been proposed to the American episcopate. This opinion is strengthened by the fact that the Eighth Provincial Council of

---

[28] Decretum Cong. de Prop. Fide, 6 Julii, 1852—*Coll. Lac.*, III, 621: "Emi Patres censuerunt permittendum . . . donec aliter a Sede Apostolica provideatur."

[29] Card. Fransoni to Archbishop Kenrick, Aug. 12, 1853—*Coll. Lac.*, III, 154.

[30] Decreta Conc. Prov. Cincin. I (1855), n. X—*Coll. Lac.*, III, 196.

[31] Instructio circa Decreta, 16 Febr., 1857—*Coll. Lac.*, III, 201. "Amplitudo tua noscit agnitum fuisse jus episcopi, ut ad sustinenda officii sui onera, ex dioecesi subsidia percipiat; applicatio tamen et determinatio subsidiorum opportunius fieri posse videtur in synodis dioecesanis, habita nimirum ratione ad uniuscujusque dioeceseos statum et conditionem."

Baltimore, which had been opened a week earlier than the Cincinnati Council, had decreed this very procedure.[32]

> Opportunum igitur videtur ut uniuscujusque dioeceseos sacerdotes, in synodo coadunati, collatis inter se consiliis, consentiant de certa pensione singulis annis Episcopo solvenda, unde officii sui munera sustentare valeat. Hac inter omnes praedictas ecclesias pro redituum ratione divisa, unaquaeque portiones suam tribuere tenebitur, dummodo tamen haec decimam pro unaquaque ecclesia redituum partem non excedat. Si autem propter ecclesiarum tenues reditus, vel parvum numerum, modus hic non sufficiat, alius idoneus pro circumstantiarum varietate excogitetur, et in illo executioni mandando boni omnes sive laici, sive clerici, auxilium praestabunt.

The essential parts of this enactment were taken over into the decrees of the Second Plenary Council of Baltimore,[33] and form the final, definite rule for the regulation of this matter. In the corrections [34] which, according to the instructions of the Sacred Congregation de Propaganda Fide, were to be made in the decrees of the Council, this statute is left unchanged, showing that it had the approval of the Holy See. In each diocese, therefore, the problem of diocesan support is to be regulated separately. The ordinary, with the help of his parochial clergy, is to decide upon the details of whatever method is to be adopted for the raising of the necessary funds. After the ordinary has approved whatever has been agreed upon, it is to be promulgated as diocesan law, and to be observed by all.

Can this diocesan assessment be called the *cathedraticum?* According to the Code,[35] which retains the interpretation that has always been attached to this word, the *cathedraticum* should be a moderate and uniform tribute, paid to the ordinary as a sign of subjection. The diocesan assessment is generally larger, is proportioned to the size and wealth of the respective benefice, and is intended to

---

[32] Acta Conc. Prov. Balt. VIII (1855), n. 7—*Coll. Lac.*, III, 162.
[33] Decreta Conc. Plen. Balt. II (1866), n. 100—*Coll. Lac.*, III, 429.
[34] Instructio de Decretis Concilii corrigendis—*Coll. Lac.*, III, 379.
[35] Can. 1504.

supply the means for the ordinary's support and for the needs of the diocese. In the available correspondence between the American episcopate and the Holy See, which led to the settling of the whole question, the word *cathedraticum* was never used. Was the avoidance of this word intentional, or not? It may serve as an indication that the Holy See prefers to retain this word in the ancient, accepted meaning. A recent decision of the Sacred Congregation of the Council [35a] supports this conclusion. Correctly considered, therefore, instead of being a *cathedraticum,* this assessment is the income of the episcopal benefice, of the *Mensa Episcopalis.*

In this country the diocesan assessment has been so generally called the *cathedraticum* that it has become customary.[36] This may have been done in a needless attempt to justify its use. The *cathedraticum* is sanctioned by the common law, while the diocesan assessment is not. But whatever may have been the reason for designating this diocesan tax as the *cathedraticum,* the Holy See has apparently given its tacit permission to this custom. The First Provincial Council of New Orleans used the word in its decree on the diocesan assessment,[37] and the Sacred Congregation of the Propaganda Fide passed this decree, without any corrections.

What the amount of the tax is to be, and in what manner it is to be levied, has been expressly referred to the judgment of the diocesan ordinary and his clergy.[38] If, as has

---

[35a] S. C. C., Dioecesis N. et Aliarum in Gallia, 13 Martii, 1920—*AAS,* XII (1920), 446.

[36] Some of the diocesan statutes, in which it was so used, are: Albany (1887), n. 202; Burlington (1886), p. 17; Hartford (1854), n. 32; Natchez (1869), n. 92; New Orleans (1858), n. 20; St. Louis (1850), n. 22; New Orleans (1889), n. 22; Wheeling (1873), n. 45; St. Louis (1929), n. 179; Syracuse (1921), n. 73.

[37] "Necessarium judicant Patres ad sacerdotum memoriam revocare jus cathedraticum Episcopis ab Ecclesia concessum, sive ad sustetandam mensam Episcopalem sive ad providendum variis dioecesis necessitatibus." Decreta Conc. Prov. Neo-Aurel. (1856), n. 11—*Coll. Lac.,* III, 242.

[38] Cf. above, footnote n. 31.

been maintained,[39] the decree of the Eighth Provincial Council of Baltimore, regarding diocesan support,[40] was drawn up according to the explicit instructions of the Holy See, the ordinary is empowered to demand one-tenth of the income of the parish, if this should be necessary. As taxable income this same decree enumerates the revenues from the renting of pews, the collections taken up during Mass, and even the offerings of the faithful on the occasion of baptisms and marriages.[41]

As the Code does not sanction this method of diocesan support, but forbids any taxes except those permitted by the law,[42] some canonists have concluded that the power of the ordinaries has been notably restricted in this matter, and that the concessions previously made are now withdrawn.[43] But this could hardly be the intention of the Holy See.[44] The diocesan assessments were also contrary to the common law that was in force before 1918.[45] Rome, however, approved of these assessments, because they offered the only practical means by which the needs of the diocese could be provided for. Necessity compelled their introduction, and it seems reasonable that, as long as this

---

39 "Everyone in the country, bishop and priest, knows that the Eighth provincial Council of Baltimore spoke the decision of Propaganda." "The Cathedraticum," *The Pastor*, V (1886), 342.

40 Decreta Conc. Prov. Balt. VIII (1855), n. 7—*Coll. Lac.*, III, 162.

41 The diocesan assessments of some of the dioceses, as prescribed in their respective statutes, have been or still are: Burlington (1886), 1/20 of the revenues from the renting of pews; Natchez (1886), 1/20 of the revenues from the renting of pews and from the collections; New Orleans (1889), 1/10 of all the rents, be they from pews or other property, also 1/10 of all collections and stole fees; and the entire collections taken up on Christmas day, Easter, and on the occasion of the administration of the Sacrament of Confirmation.

42 Canons 1505 and 1506.

43 Vermeersch-Creusen, *Epitome, I. C.*, II, n. 826: "Ante Codicem, permittebant episcopo, non solum ut cathedraticum exigeret, sed etiam ut certam contributionem imponeret ecclesiis pro propria sustentatione et communibus dioecesis expensis, in regionibus in quibus reditus stabiles in hunc finem non haberet. Hodie autem valde circumscripta est potestas episcopi canonibus 1505 et 1506."

44 Ayrinhac, *Administrative Legislation in the New Code of Canon Law*, p. 402.

45 "The Cathedraticum," *The Pastor*, V (1886), 337.

necessity continues, they may also be allowed to continue, unless the Holy See expressly rules otherwise.

Recourse is often had to special collections to provide for certain diocesan and extra-diocesan needs of the Church. The local ordinary specifies a certain Sunday or Holy-day on which a collection is to be taken up at all the Masses for whatever purpose he has prescribed. The faithful are generally informed on one or more preceding Sundays that this collection will be for the specified work, and are asked to contribute accordingly. Four special collections, which are held in practically all the dioceses of the country, are:

1. The Peter's Pence. In the Second Plenary Council of Baltimore the bishops of the country decided [46] that a collection was to be taken up each year in every church for the needs of the Holy Father.

2. For the support of the Church in the Holy Land. In a letter of December 26th, 1887,[47] Pope Leo XIII prescribed that a collection was to be taken up for this purpose, at least once a year, in every parish church throughout the world. In this country the contributions, which are made on Good Friday, are ordinarily intended for this purpose.

3. For the Catholic University of America. The Fathers of the Third Plenary Council of Baltimore, after decreeing that the University was to be founded as soon as possible, urged the faithful to contribute towards its support.[48] An annual collection for this purpose has become customary in practically all dioceses.

4. For the Indian and Negro Missions. This collection was prescribed by the Third Plenary Council of Baltimore.[49] At the present time it is often combined with the collection that is taken up for missions in foreign fields and is known as the collection for Home and Foreign Missions.

In various dioceses collections are also taken up for other purposes, such as the support of diocesan schools, semin-

[46] Decreta Conc. Plen. Balt. II (1866), n. 48—*Coll. Lac.*, III, 412.
[47] *ASS*, XX, 419.
[48] Decreta Conc. Plen. Balt. III (1884), n. 183 and 184.
[49] Decreta Conc. Plen. Balt. III (1884), n. 243.

aries, charitable institutions, particular missions, etc. In regard to these special collections, a few general principles may be stated.

1. Since the local ordinary holds a public office in the Church, he can, within the limits of his territory, collect alms without having to obtain permission from anyone.[50] This right to collect alms also includes the right to take up collections during public services. It is explicitly given to the pastors of parishes, by the common law.[51] As the ordinary and immediate pastor of the entire diocese,[52] the local ordinary, especially if he be the residential bishop, enjoys this same right to a higher degree. He can also demand that the clergy subject to him assist him in gathering these alms. He can prescribe when and what announcements are to be made of such collections in the parishes, and when and in what manner they are to be taken up.

2. Subject to the power of eminent domain which the Holy See enjoys, donations belong to that moral person to whom the donor intended that they be given.[53] If then such a special collection has been announced and taken up, the pastor of the parish must turn over all the contributions made by the faithful to this special collection. This does not always mean that the entire collection of that day must be sent in. In some places it is understood, either as the result of a custom, or through diocesan regulations,[54] that the church will retain an amount equal to the ordinary Sunday collection, and send in the remainder. This practice is followed, and permitted by ordinaries, especially in such places where the Offertory collections are the chief source of revenues for the parish. The faithful, however, have to know of this arrangement, otherwise it must be held that whatever they contribute is contributed for the particular purpose for which the collection is held.

---

[50] Canon 1503.

[51] Canon 415, §2, 5°, and 630, §4.

[52] Canon 334.

[53] Canon 1499, §2; cf. also Leo XIII, const. "*Romanos Pontifices,*" die 8 Maii, 1881, §26: "Namque receptum est hac in re, spectari primum oportere quid largitor voluerit."—*Fontes*, III, n. 582, p. 183.

[54] E.g., Decreta Synodi Dioec. Sti. Ludovici Septimae (1929), n. 164, B.

Before, however, announcing such an arrangement to the people, the pastor should consult his ordinary. It may be the latter's intention that the regular Sunday collection is to be omitted entirely on that day, so that whatever is received is to be considered as donated for the particular purpose for which the special collection is held. Even if the ordinary permits such a division, he may except certain collections from this arrangement. Thus, the statutes of the diocese of St. Louis, which explicitly permit such a division,[55] prescribe that the entire collection for Peter's Pence, as also for orphanages and seminaries, is to be sent in.[56]

3. Any donations, which are explicitly intended for some specific purpose, must be sent by the pastor to the proper person, without any diminution. This follows from what has been said above.[57]

---

[55] Decreta Syn. Dioec. Sti. Ludovici Septimae (1929), n. 164, B.

[56] *Ibidem*, n. 164, C.

[57] A more detailed exposition of these principles is to be found in the *Amer. Ecc. Rev.*, LXXIX, 15 et seq., "Peter's Pence, Catholic University and Foreign Mission Collections," by Dr. Philip Bernardini.

BIBLIOGRAPHY

SOURCES

Acta Apostolicae Sedis (*AAS*), Romae, 1909-

Acta Sanctae Sedis (*ASS*), 41 vols., Romae, 1865-1908.

Acta et Decreta Concilii Plenarii Baltimorensis III, Baltimorae, 1886.

Acta et Decreta Conciliorum Recentiorum (*Collectio Lacensis*), 7 vols., Friburgi Brisgoviae, 1870-1890.

Ante-Nicene Christian Library, Translations of the writings of the Fathers down to A. D. 325, ed. by Rev. A. Roberts and James Donaldson, Vol. XVII, Edinburgh, 1870.

Canones et Decreta Concilii Tridentini, 19 ed., Taurini, 1913.

Codex Iuris Canonici Pii X Pontificis Maximi iussu digestus, Benedicti Papae XV, auctoritate promulgatus, Romae, 1918.

Codex Theodosianus, ed. P. Krueger, Th. Mommsen, P. M. Meyer, 3 vols., Berolini, 1905.

Codicis Iuris Canonici Fontes, cura Emi. Petri Card. Gasparri editi, 4 vols., Romae, 1926-

Collectanea Sacrae Congregationis de Propaganda Fide (*Coll.*), 2 vols., Romae, 1907.

Corpus Iuris Canonici, ed. Richter-Friedberg, 2 vols., Lipsiae, 1922.

Corpus Iuris Civilis, ed. P. Krueger, Berolini, 1922.

Diocesan Statutes—Albany, 1887; Altoona, 1923; Boston, 1919; Buffalo, 1924; Burlington, 1886; Crookston, 1921; Harrisburg, 1928; Hartford, 1854; Los Angeles, 1927; Louisville, 1874 and 1896; Natchez, 1869 and 1886; New Orleans, 1858 and 1889; New York, 1842; Oklahoma, 1913; Philadelphia, 1842; St. Cloud, 1924; St. Louis, 1850 and 1929; San Francisco, 1862; Syracuse, 1921; Wheeling, 1893.

Mansi, Joannes, *Sacrorum Conciliorum Nova et Amplissima Collectio*, 53 vols., Parisiis, 1901-1927.

Missale Romanum, Editio III, juxta Typicam Vaticanam, Ratisbonae, 1920.

Raccolta di Concordati, su Materie Ecclesiastiche tra la Santa Sede e le Autorita Civili, Romae, 1919.

Religious Bodies, United States Department of Commerce, Bureau of the Census, Washington, 1929.

The Official Catholic Year Book, Anno Domini, 1928, New York.

WORKS OF REFERENCE

Alzog, Rev. John, *Manual of Universal Church History*, 3 vols., translated, with additions, from the Ninth and last German Edition by F. J. Pabisch and Rev. Thos. B. Byrne; Cincinnati, Robt. Clarke & Co., 1878.

Ayrinhac, Rev. H. A., S.S., *Administrative Legislation in the New Code of Canon Law*, New York, Longmans Green & Co., 1930.

Babelon, Ernest, *Traité des Monnaies Grecques et Romanais*, Vol. I, Part. I, Paris, 1907.

[Bachofen] Augustine, Rev. P. Chas., O.S.B., *A Commentary on the New Code of Canon Law*, 8 vols., St. Louis, B. Herder Book Co., 1921-1925.

————*Rights and Duties of Ordinaries according to the Code and Apostolic Faculties*, St. Louis, 1924.

————*The Pastor according to the New Code of Canon Law*, 3 ed., St. Louis, 1926.

Bardenhewer, Otto, *Patrology, the Lives and Works of the Fathers of the Church*, translated from the second edition by Thomas J. Shahan, St. Louis, 1908.

Beard, Chas. A. & Mary R., *The Rise of American Civilization*, 2 vols., One Volume Ed., New York, Macmillan Co., 1930.

Belloc, Hilaire, *Europe and the Faith*, New York, 1920.

————*How the Reformation Happened*, New York. 1928.

Bingham, Joseph, *Antiquities of the Christian Church*, 2 vols., London, 1856.

Cappello, Felix M., *De Visitatione SS. Liminum et Dioeceseon, ac De Relatione S. Sedi exhibenda*, 2 vols., Romae, Pustet, 1913.

Catholic Encyclopedia, 17 vols., New York, 1907-1922.

Clarke, Rev. Henry W., *A History of Tithes*, London and New York, Scribners and Co., 1894.

Cocchi, G., *Commentarium in Codicem Iuris Canonici*, 6 vols., Augustae Taurinorum, 1921.

Creighton, Mandel, *A History of the Papacy During the Period of the Reformation*, 2 vols., London, 1892.

Davis, Wm. Stearns, *Life in a Medieval Barony, A Picture of a Typical Feudal Community in the Thirteenth Century*, New York, Harper Bros., 1923.

DeMeester, A., *Iuris Canonici et Iuris Canonico-Civilis Compendium*, 3 vols., Brugis, 1921-1928.

Denzinger, H.-Bannwart, C., *Enchiridion Symbolorum Definitionum et Declarationum*, 13 ed., Friburgi Brisgoviae, 1921.

Doheny, Wm. J., C.S.C., *Church Property, Modes of Acquisition*, Washington, D. C., 1927.

Eichmann, Eduard, *Lehrbuch des Kirchenrechts*, 2 ed., Paderborn, 1926.

Fitton, James, *Sketches of the Establishment of the Church in New England*, Boston, 1872.

Foakes-Jackson, F. J., *History of the Christian Church up to 461*, New York, 1924.

Funk, F. X., *Lehrbuch der Kirchengeschichte*, 2 vols. (increased and revised by Dr. Karl Bihlmeyer), Paderborn, 1921.

Gasquet, Abbot, *Parish Life in Medieval England*, Chicago, Benziger Brothers, 1906.

Godfrey, John A., *The Right of Patronage According to the Code of Canon Law*, Washington, D. C., 1924.

Grisar, Hartmann, S.J., *History of Rome and the Popes in the Middle Ages*, Authorized English Translation by Luigi Cappadelta, 3 vols., London, 1911.

Grünewald, J., *Die Rechtsverhältnisse an Kirchenstühlen*, Paderborn, 1927.

Hilling, Nikolaus, *Das Sachenrecht des Codex Iuris Canonici*, Freiburg i. Br., 1928.

Hope, Mrs., *S. Boniface and the Conversion of Germany*, London, 1872.

Johnson, Vernon, *One Lord, One Faith*, New York, 1929.

Kenrick, F., *Theologia Moralis*, Philadelphia, 1842.

Kurth-Godefroid, *The Church at the Turning Points of History*, Translated from the French by the Rt. Rev. Victor Day, Helena, Mont., 1918.

Link, *Mess-Stipendien*, Regensburg, 1901.

MacCaffrey, Rev. James, *History of the Catholic Church from the Renaissance to the French Revolution*, 2 vols., St. Louis, 1915.

Maes, Rev. Camillus P., *The Life of Father Nerinckx*, Cincinnati, 1880.

Maroto, P., *Institutiones Iuris Canonici*, 2 vols., Romae, 1919-1921.

MPG=*Migne, Patrologia Graeca.*

MPL=*Migne, Patrologia Latina.*

Milman, Henry, *The History of Christianity from the Birth of Christ to the Abolition of Paganism in the Roman Empire*, 3 vols., New York, 1887.

Noldin, H., S.J., *Summa Theologiae Moralis*, 3 vols., 16 ed., Ratisbonae et Neo Eboraci, 1923.

Platz, Herman, *Geistige Kämpfe im modernen Frankreich*, München, 1922.

Pöschl, Arnold, *Bischofsgut und Mensa Episcopalis*, 3 vols., Bonn, 1908-1912.

Prümmer, Dominicus, *Manuale Iuris Canonici*, 3 ed., Friburgi Brisgoviae, 1922.

Ratzinger, P., *Geschichte der kirchenlichen Armenpflege*, Freiburg im Breisgau, 1884.

Schmalzgrueber, Franciscus, *Jus Ecclesiasticum Universum*, 12 vols., Romae, 1843-1845.

Shea, John G., *A History of the Catholic Church in the United States*, 4 vols., New York, 1892.

Sozomen, *The Ecclesiastical History of*, Translated from the Greek by Edward Walford, London, 1855.

Suarez, Franciscus, *Opera Omnia*, 26 vols., Paris, 1861.
The Diocese of St. Paul, the Golden Jubilee, St. Paul, 1901.
Thomas Aquinas, *Summa Theologica*, Taurini, 1917.
Thomassinus, L., *Vetus et Nova Disciplina Ecclesiae circa Beneficia et Beneficiarios*, Magontiaci, 1787.
Vermeersch-Creusen, *Epitome Iuris Canonici*, 3 ed., 3 vols., Mechlinae-Romae, 1927-1928.
Vogt, Joseph, *Das kirchliche Vermögensrecht*, Cöln, 1910.
Wall, J. Charles, *An Old English Parish*, London, 1907.
Walsh, James J., *The Thirteenth Greatest of Centuries*, New York, 1910.
Wernz, F. X., *Ius Decretalium*, 6 vols., Romae, 1908-1913.
Woywod, S., *A Practical Commentary of the Code of Canon Law*, 2 vols., New York, 1925.

PERIODICALS

Acolyte, The, Huntington, Indiana, 1925-
America, The, New York, 1909-
American Catholic Quarterly Review, Philadelphia, 1876-
American Ecclesiastical Review, Philadelphia, 1889-
Archiv für katholisches Kirchenrecht (*AkKR*), Mainz, 1857-
Commonweal, New York, 1924-
Dublin Review, Dublin, 1837-
Hispanic-American Historical Review, Baltimore, 1918-
Homiletic and Pastoral Review, New York, 1900-
Irish Ecclesiastical Record, Dublin, 1867-
Month, The, London, 1852-
Pastor, The, New York, 1882-1888.
Theologisch-praktische Quartalschrift (*LQS*), Linz, 1832-

UNIVERSITAS CATHOLICA AMERICAE

WASHINGTON, D. C.

FACULTAS IURIS CANONICI

1930

No. 61

DEUS LUX MEA

TITULI

QUOS

AD DOCTORATUS GRADUM

IN

IURE CANONICO

APUD UNIVERSITATEM CATHOLICAM AMERICAE

CONSEQUENDUM

PUBLICE PROPUGNABIT

MICHAEL NICOLAUS KREMER

SACERDOS DIOECESIS SANCTI CLODOALDI

IURIS CANONICI LICENTIATUS

HORA IX A. M. DIE XXVII MAII A. D. MCMXXX

TITULI

IN IURE CANONICO

I.	De Dissertatione.	
II.	De Historia Iuris Canonici.	
III.	Canones 1-7	De Ambitu Codicis.
IV.	Canones 8-24	De Legibus Ecclesiasticis.
V.	Canones 25-30	De Consuetudine.
VI.	Canones 31-35	De Temporis Supputatione.
VII.	Canones 36-62	De Rescriptis.
VIII.	Canones 63-79	De Privilegiis.
IX.	Canones 80-86	De Dispensationibus.
X.	Canones 87-107	Generales Notiones de Personis.
XI.	Canones 111-117	De Clericorum Adscriptione Alicui Dioecesi.
XII.	Canones 118-123	De Iuribus et Privilegiis Clericorum.
XIII.	Canones 124-144	De Obligationibus Clericorum.
XIV.	Canones 145-195	De Officiis Ecclesiasticis.
XV.	Canones 196-210	De Potestate Ordinaria et Delegata.
XVI.	Canones 487-498	De Notione Religionis, et de Erectione et Suppressione Religionis, Provinciae, Domus.
XVII.	Canones 499-537	De Religionum Regimine.
XVIII.	Canones 538-586	De Admissione in Religionem.
XIX.	Canones 587-591	De Ratione Studiorum in Religionibus Clericalibus.
XX.	Canones 592-631	De Obligationibus et Privilegiis Religiosorum.
XXI.	Canones 632-672	De Transitu ad Aliam Religionem, de Egressu e Religione, et de Dimissione Religiosorum.
XXII.	Canones 673-681	De Societatibus sive Virorum sive Mulierum in Communi Viventium sine Votis.
XXIII.	Canones 1012-1018	De Matrimonio in Genere.
XXIV.	Canones 1019-1034	De Iis quae Matrimonii Celebrationi Praemitti debent.
XXV.	Canones 1035-1057	De Impedimentis in Genere.
XXVI.	Canones 1058-1066	De Impedimentis Impedientibus.
XXVII.	Canones 1067-1080	De Impedimentis Dirimentibus.

XXVIII.	Canones 1081-1093	De Consensu Matrimoniali.
XXIX.	Canones 1552-1568	De Notione Iudicii et de Foro Competenti.
XXX.	Canones 1569-1607	De Variis Tribunalium Gradibus et Speciebus.
XXXI.	Canones 1608-1645	De Disciplina in Tribunalibus Servanda.
XXXII.	Canones 1646-1666	De Partibus in Causa.
XXXIII.	Canones 1667-1705	De Actionibus et Exceptionibus.
XXXIV.	Canones 1706-1725	De Causae Introductione.
XXXV.	Canones 1726-1746	De Litis Contestatione, de Litis Instantia, et de Interrogationibus Partibus in Iudicio Faciendis.
XXXVI.	Canones 1747-1836	De Probationibus.
XXXVII.	Canones 1837-1857	De Causis Incidentibus.
XXXVIII.	Canones 1858-1877	De Processus Publicatione, de Conclusione in Causa, de Causae Discussione, et de Sententia.
XXXIX.	Canones 2195-2198	De Natura Delicti eiusque Divisione.
XL.	Canones 2199-2211	De Imputabilitate Delicti, de Causis illam Aggravantibus vel Minuentibus, et de Iuridicis Delicti Effectibus.
XLI.	Canones 2212-2213	De Conatu Delicti.
XLII.	Canones 2214-2240	De Poenis in Genere.
XLIII.	Canones 2241-2285	De Poenis Medicinalibus seu de Censuris.
XLIV.	Canones 2286-2305	De Poenis Vindicativis.
XLV.	Canones 2306-2313	De Remediis Poenalibus et Poenitentiis.

IN IURE ROMANO

XLVI. The Periods of Roman Law.
XLVII. The Sources of Roman Law.
XLVIII. Personality.
XLIX. Slavery.
L. Citizenship.
LI. Patria Potestas.
LII. Personae in Manu.
LIII. Tutela et Cura.
LIV. Personae in Mancipio.
LV. Ownership.
LVI. De Obligationibus in Genere.
LVII. De Obligationibus Extra-Contractualibus.

LVIII. Furtum.
LIX. Damnum Injuria Datum.
LX. Injuria.

Vidit Facultas:

PHILIPPUS BERNARDINI, S.T.D., J.U.D., Decanus.
LUDOVICUS H. MOTRY, S.T.D., J.C.D., a Secretis.
VALENTINUS T. SCHAAF, O.F.M., J.C.D.
FRANCISCUS J. LARDONE, S.T.D., J.U.D.

Vidit Rector Magnificus Universitatis:

JACOBUS HUGO RYAN, Ph.D., S.T.D.

BIOGRAPHICAL NOTE

Michael N. Kremer was born December 16, 1898, at Watkins, Minnesota. After a grade school education at that place, he attended St. Lawrence College, Mt. Calvary, Wisconsin, from 1913 to 1918. He prepared for the priesthood at St. John's University, Collegeville, Minnesota, where he received the degree of Bachelor of Arts in 1920. Upon the completion of his theological studies he received the degree of Bachelor of Sacred Theology from the Catholic University. He was ordained to the Holy Priesthood on June 1, 1924. After four years of work in the diocese of St. Cloud he was sent by Bishop Busch to the Catholic University for graduate studies in the School of Canon Law.

www.ingramcontent.com/pod-product-compliance
Lightning Source LLC
LaVergne TN
LVHW050210080826
844660LV00012B/391

* 9 7 8 0 8 1 3 2 2 2 5 0 9 *